AF322977

Art to Hear

Masks. Metamorphoses of the Face
From Rodin to Picasso

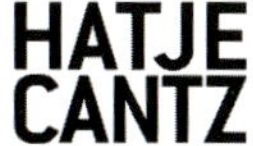
HATJE
CANTZ

MATHILDENHÖHE
DARMSTADT

Contents

Since the mask reveals by concealing, and disguises while showing, it touches the core of humans, and of life itself. While, during antiquity, the mask's central importance was as ritual object as well as theater prop, since the mid-nineteenth century, it has enjoyed a remarkable renaissance. Its "disturbing strangeness" offers outstanding experiential richness and a means of aesthetic renewal.

Around 1900, with its suggestive power, the mask ignites the imagination of numerous sculptors, painters, and photographers. The recollection of the mask's classical role is always present, but ancient archetypes such as the gorgon head of Medusa or the Christian *topoi* such as John the Baptist's severed head are increasingly displaced by contemporary influences, for instance, of Japanese art.

The mask is as well inseparably connected to the principle of fragmentation, which gives new fundamental impulses to sculpture at the turn of the century. The architectural decor of Art Nouveau brings new life to the old adornments of the mascarons. At the beginning of the twentieth century, when so-called primitive masks from Africa and Oceania enjoy great popularity, the artistic occupation with the mask moves toward a very own, now eminently modern direction.

On the basis of about forty masterpieces from different cultures, dating particularly from 1860 to 1930, this audio guide tells us about the eminent experiments and fantastic findings about the form of masks. A statement by Claude Lévi-Strauss completes the picture. This accompanying volume presents the annotated works of Auguste Rodin, Paul Gauguin, Arnold Böcklin, and others in large-format color illustrations.

"A mask tells us more than a face."
OSCAR WILDE

52 pages   44 plates   CD running time: 80 min.

CD Index

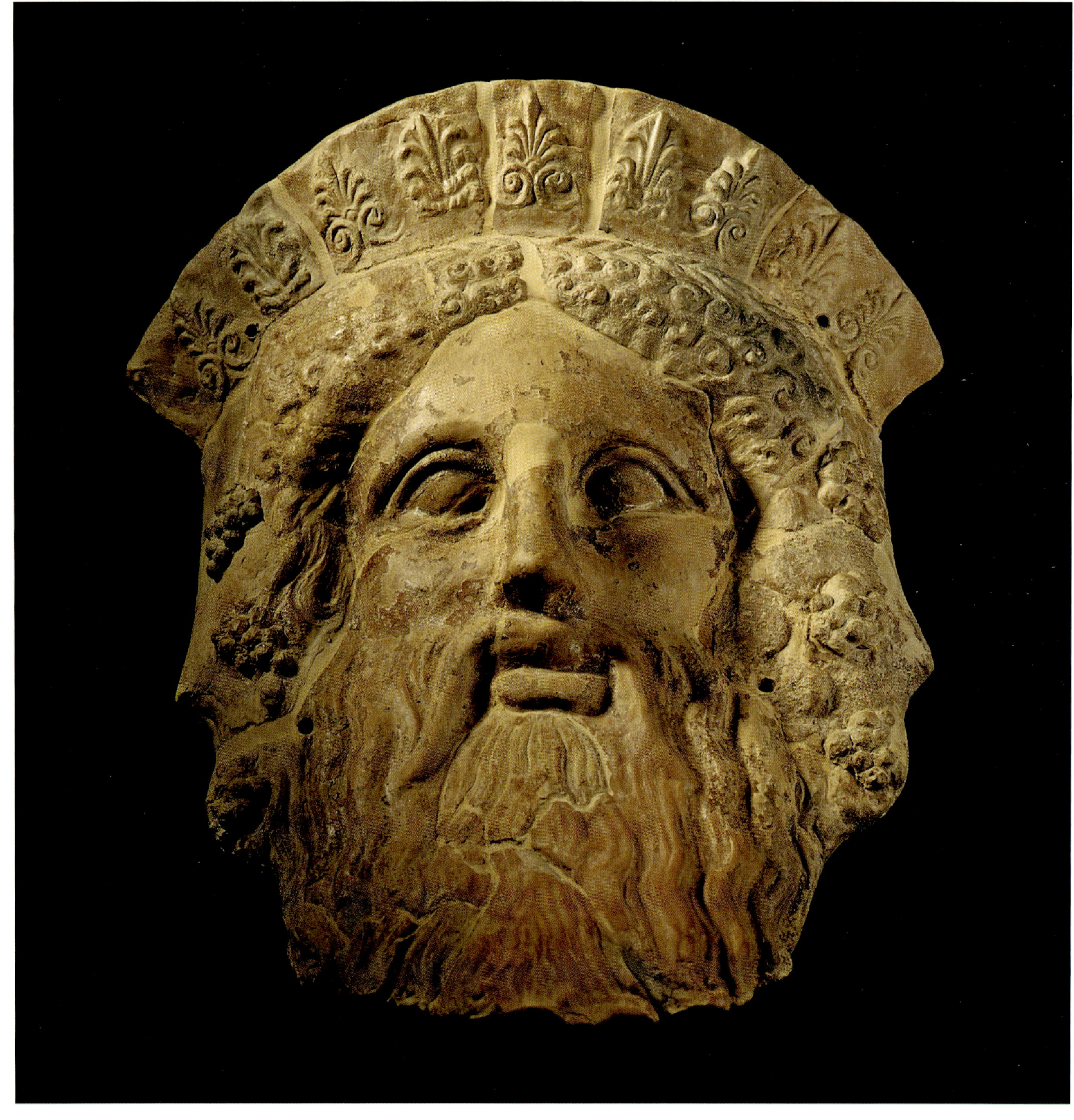

6 ▷ 2 **Greece (Boeotia)** Mask of Dionysus 450–400 BC, terracotta cast, Musée du Louvre, Paris

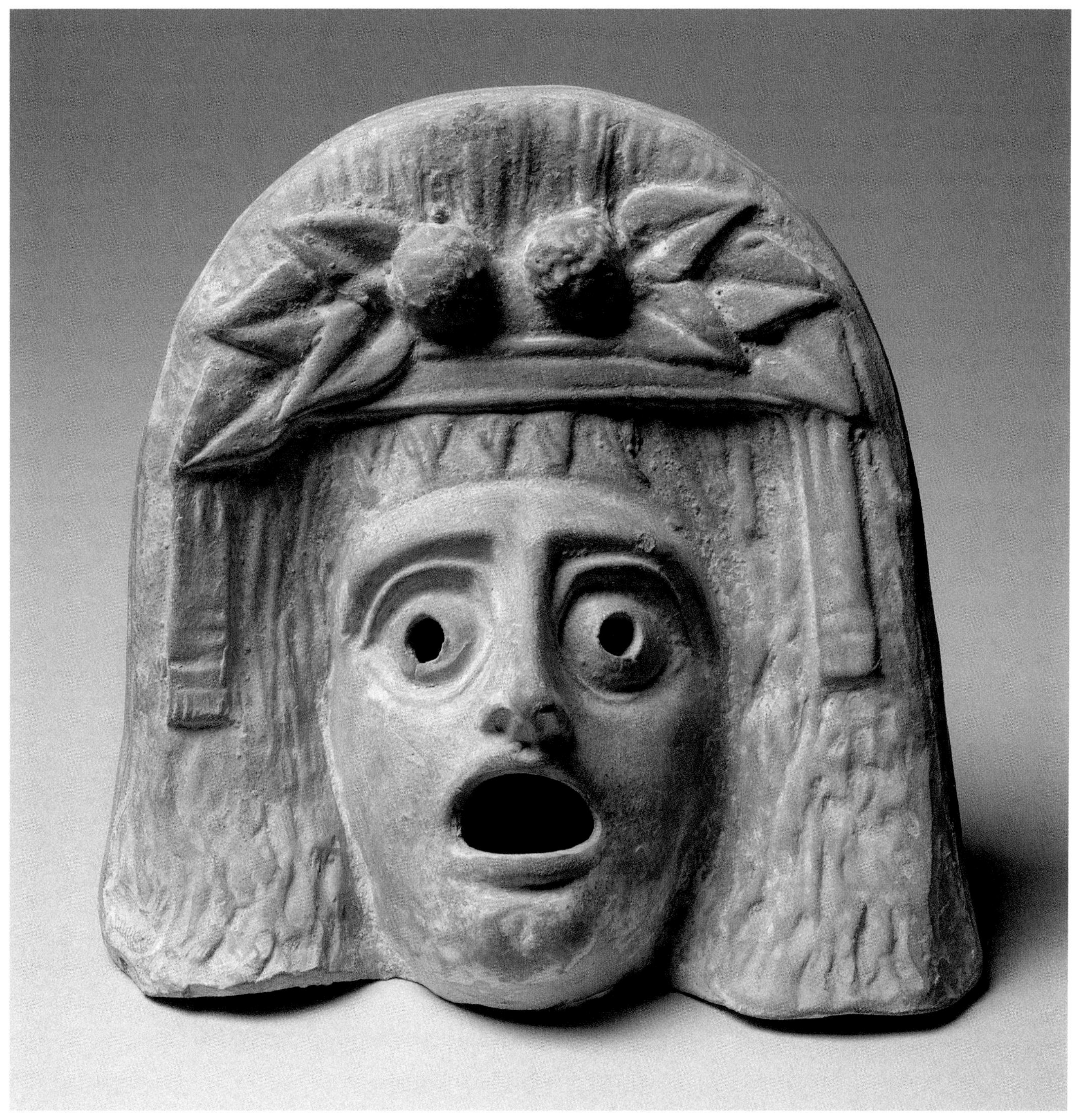

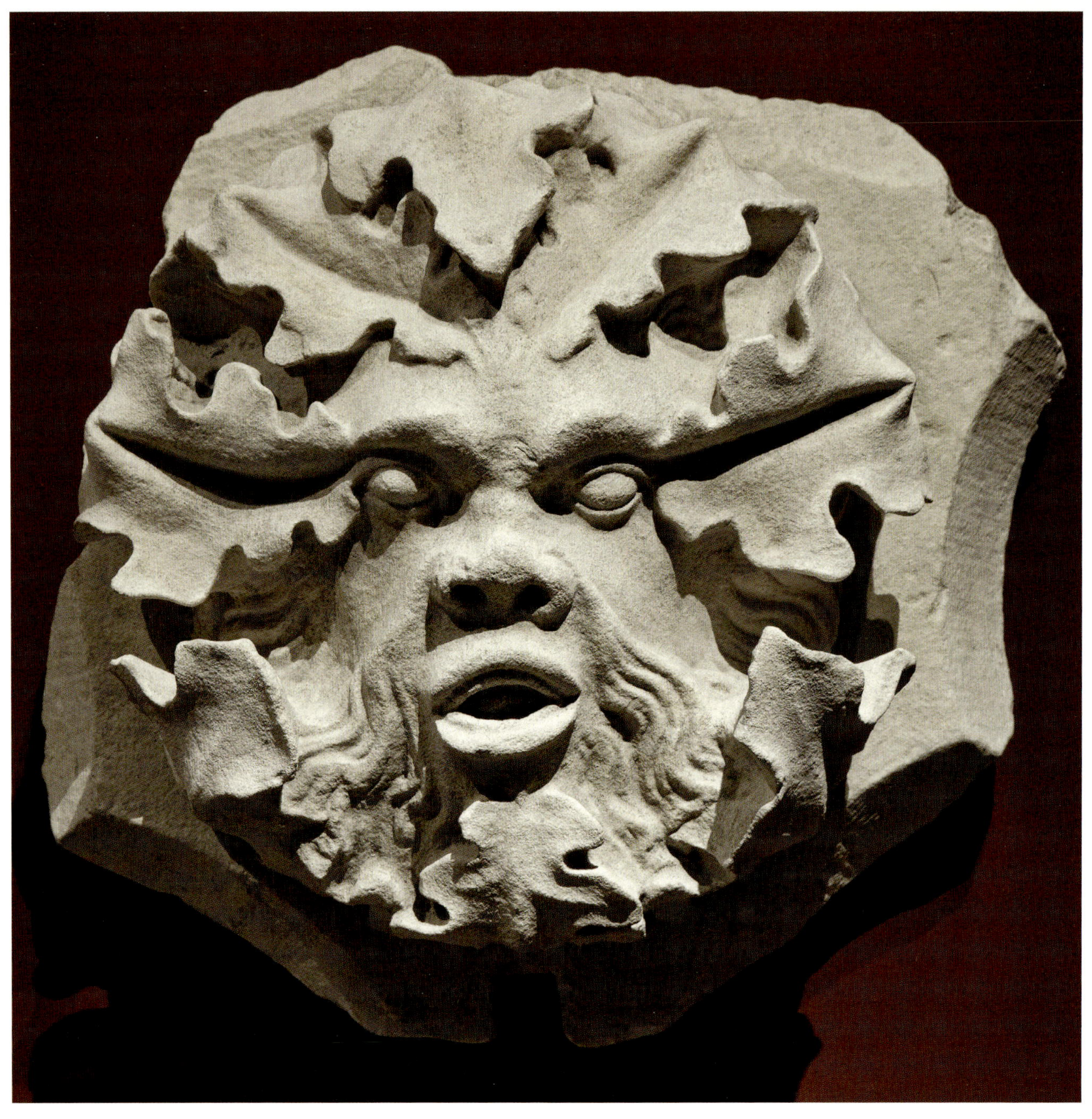

▷ 3 France (Île-de-France)   Foliate Head (architectural fragment)
Fourteenth century, marble, Musée National du Moyen Âge –
Thermes et Hôtel de Cluny, Paris

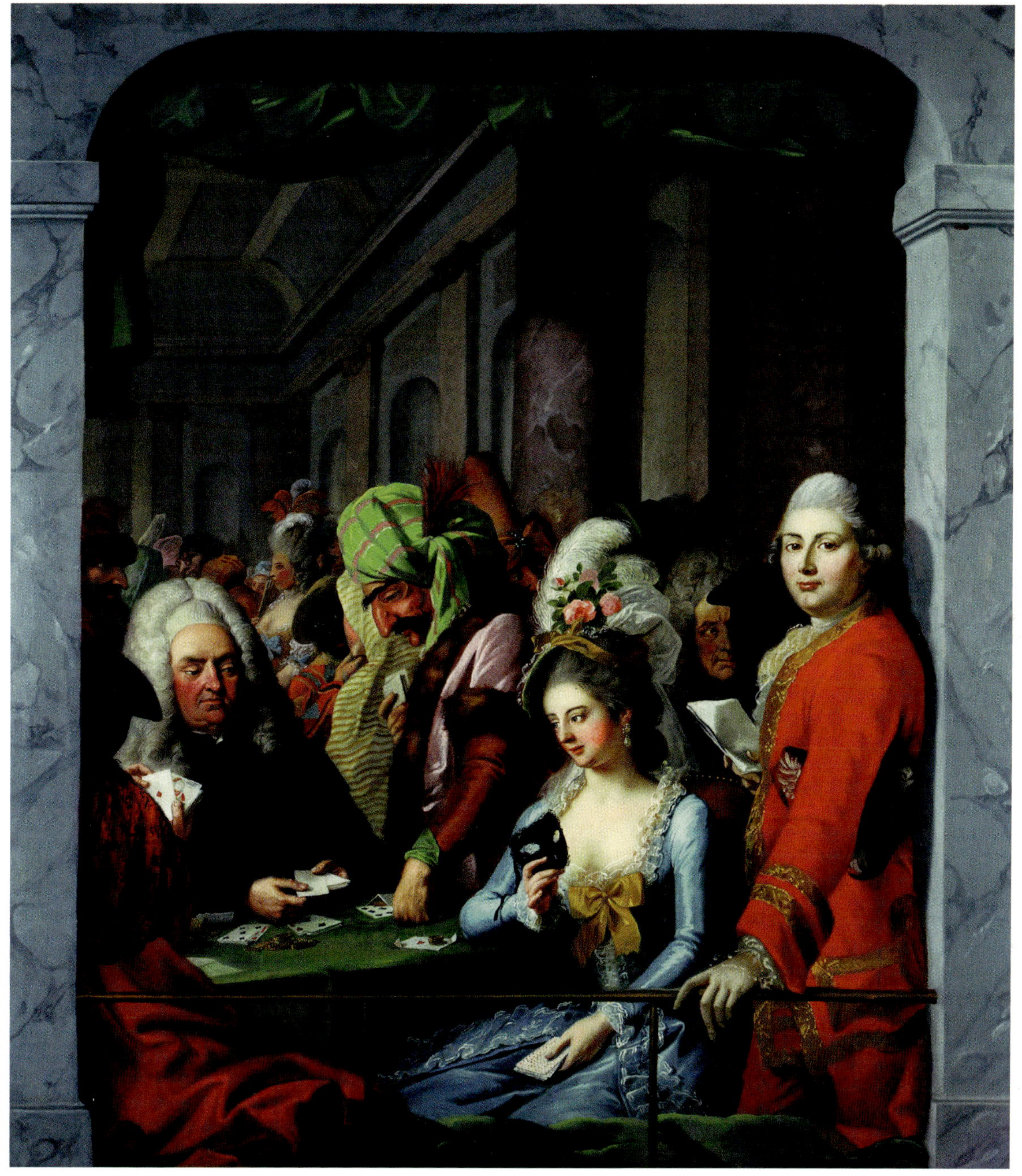

▷ 4   Johann Heinrich Tischbein   Mask Scene with Characters from Kassel
1780/85, oil on canvas, Museumslandschaft Hessen Kassel,
Gemäldegalerie Alte Meister, Kassel

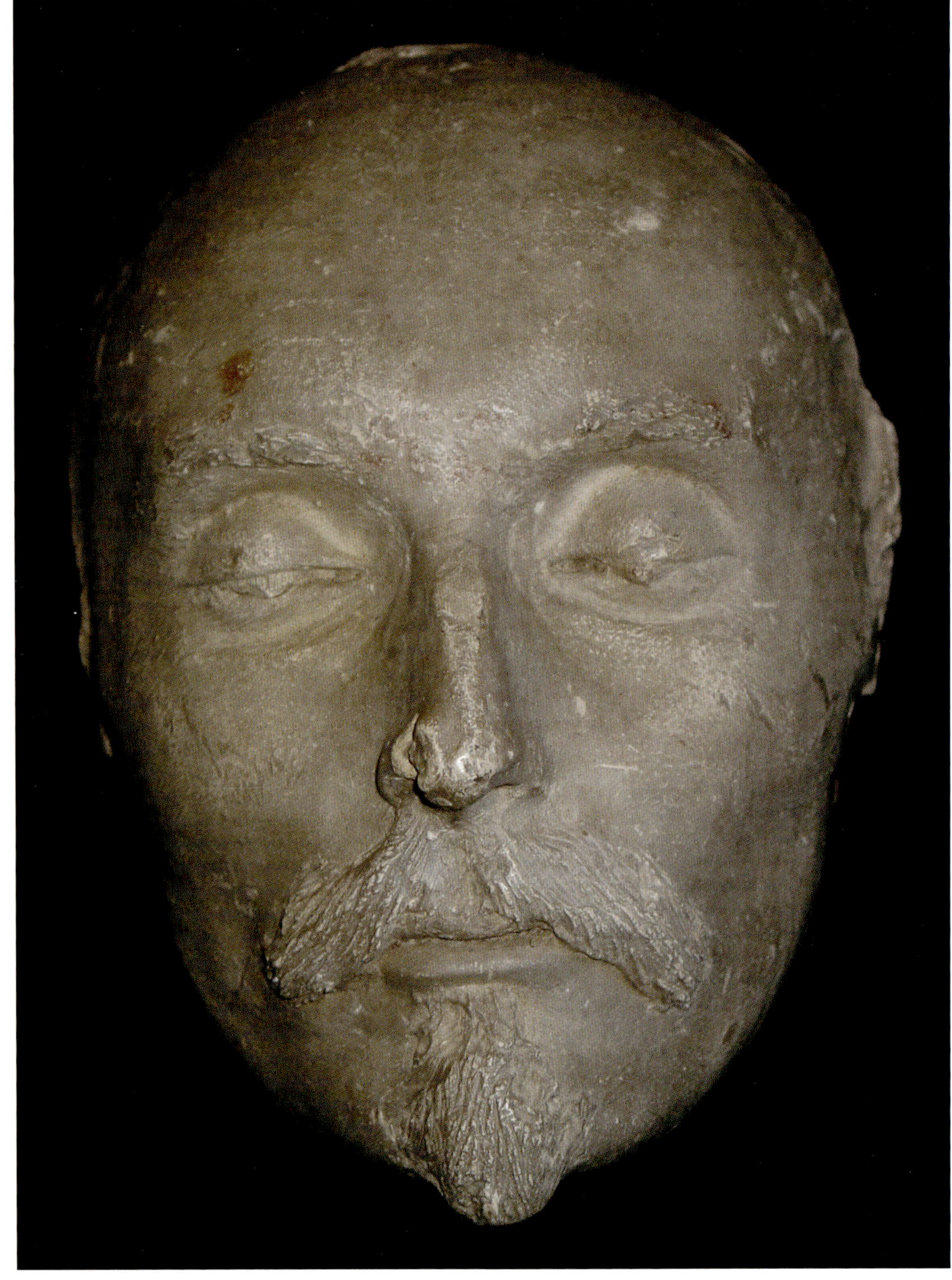

 ▷ 5 **England** Shakespeare's Death Mask 1616, plaster, Städtische Kunstsammlung, Institut Mathildenhöhe Darmstadt

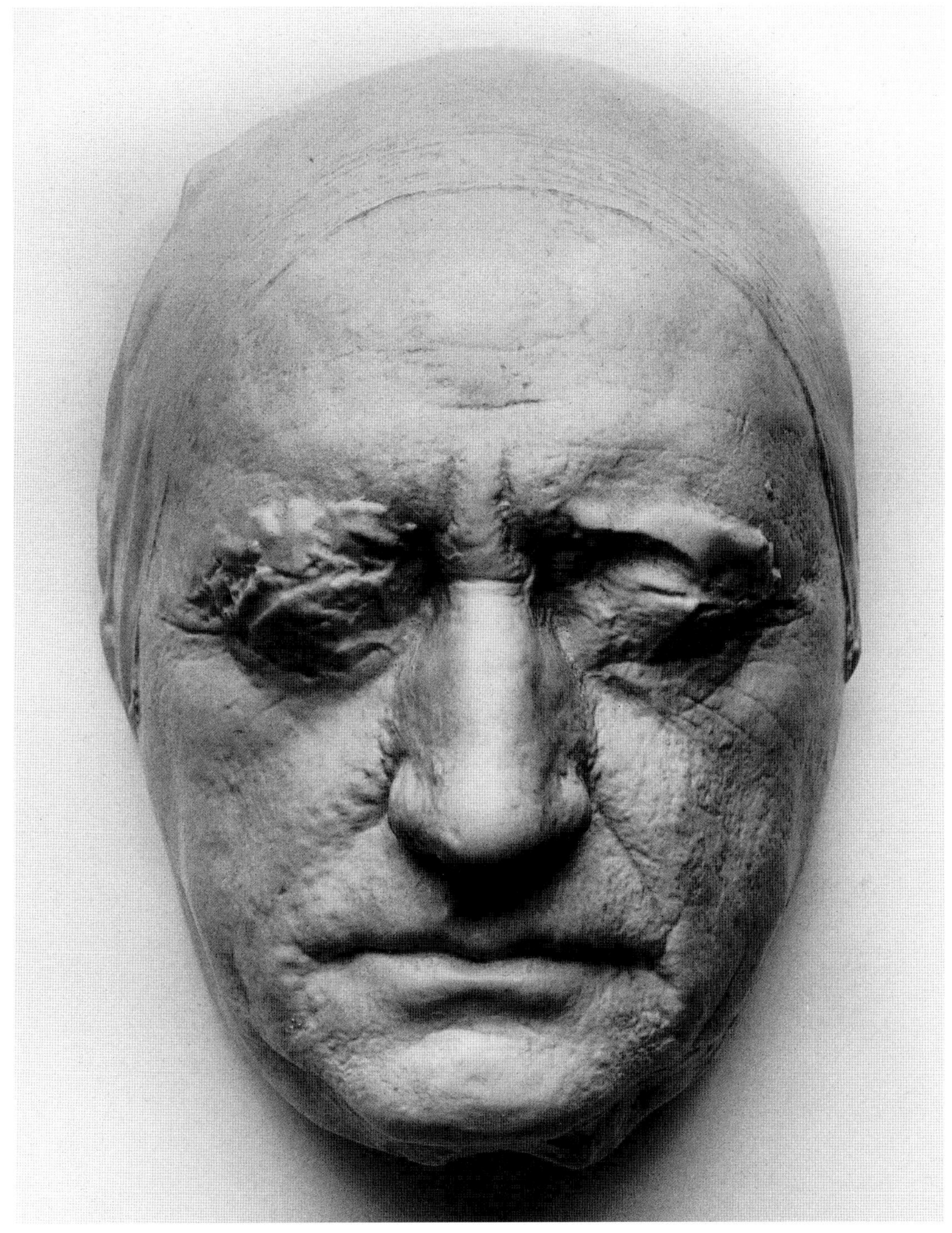

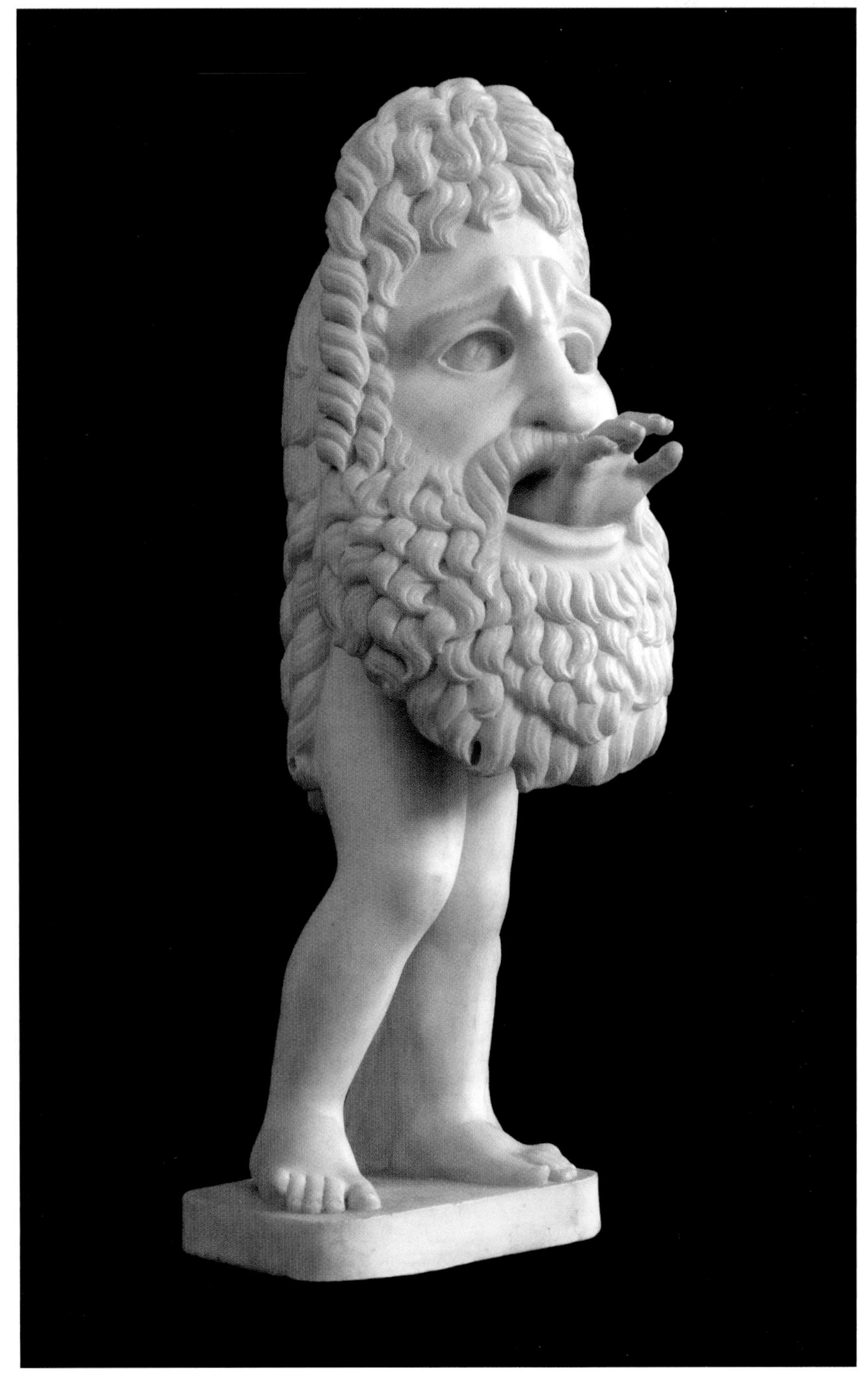

▷ 6 Bartolomeo Cavaceppi (attributed to)   Child Hiding behind a Mask (also known as False Amor)
1799, marble, Collection T. Longstaffe-Gowan and T. Knox, London

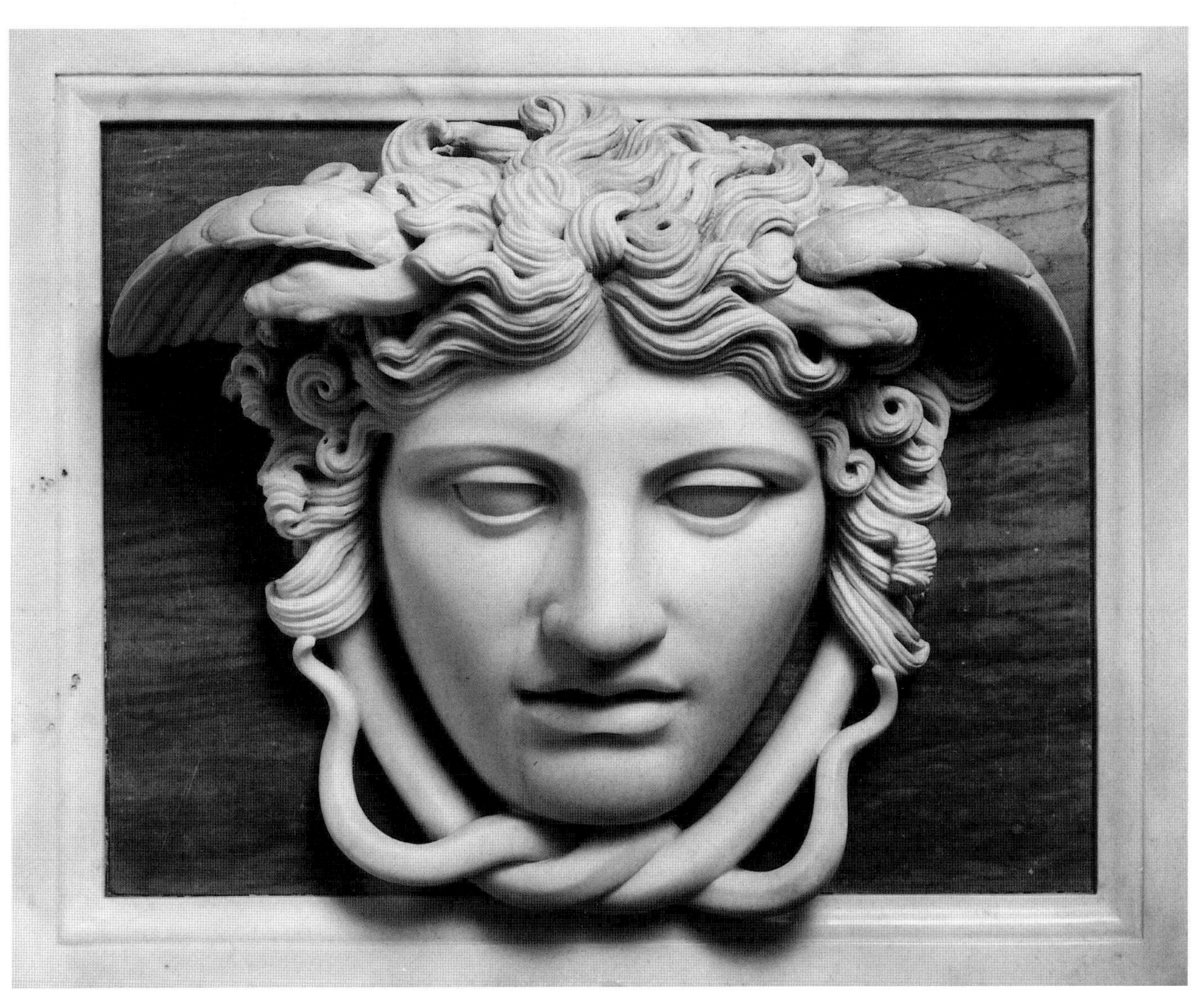

▷ 7   **Italy**   Copy of "Medusa Rondanini"
Ca. 1800, marble, Ny Carlsberg Glyptotek, Copenhagen

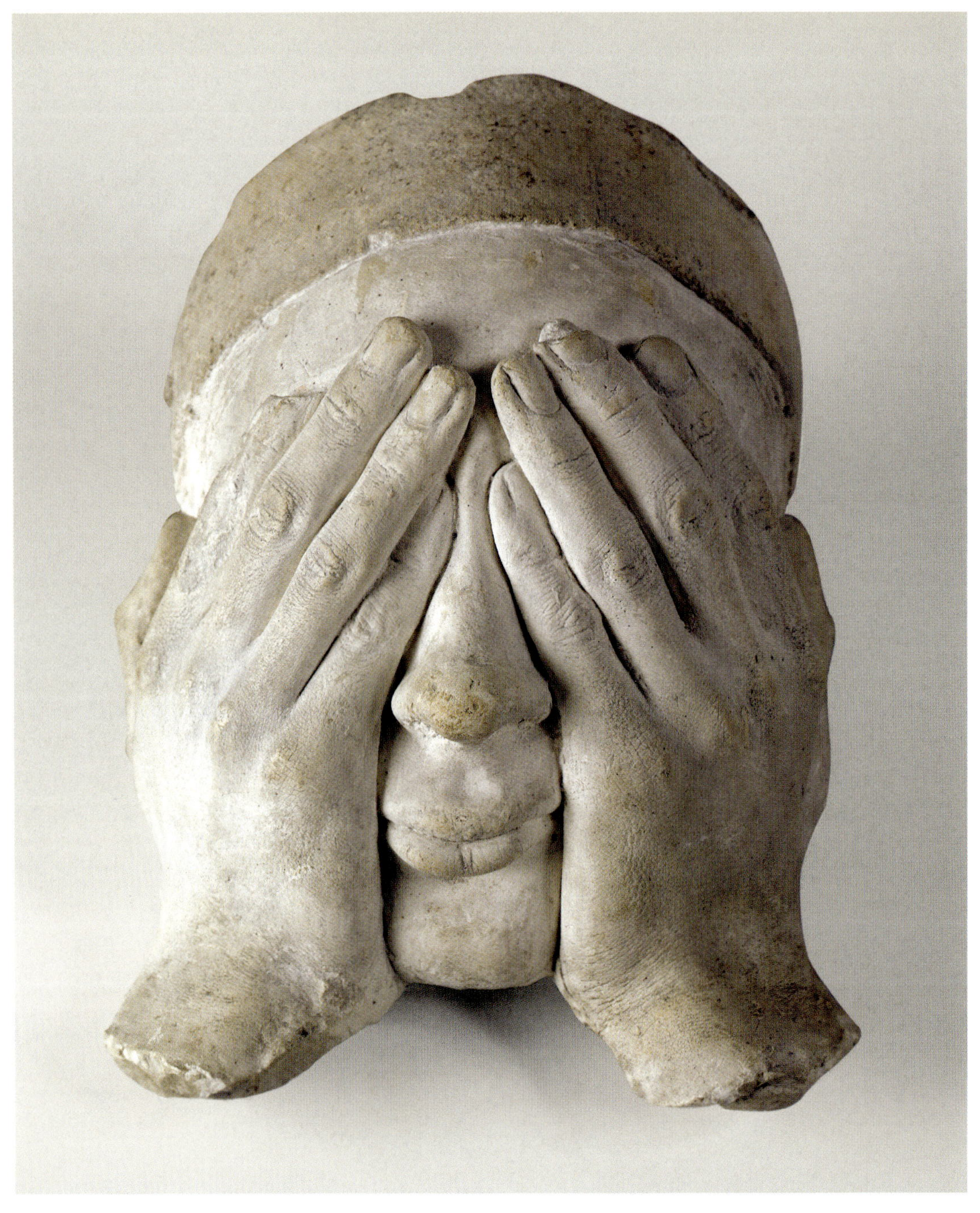

▷ 8   Adolphe-Victor Geoffroy-Dechaume   Plaster Cast of Louis Steinheil's Face, Covering His Eyes with His Hands
1834, plaster, Musée des Monuments Français – Cité de l'Architecture
et du Patrimoine, Paris

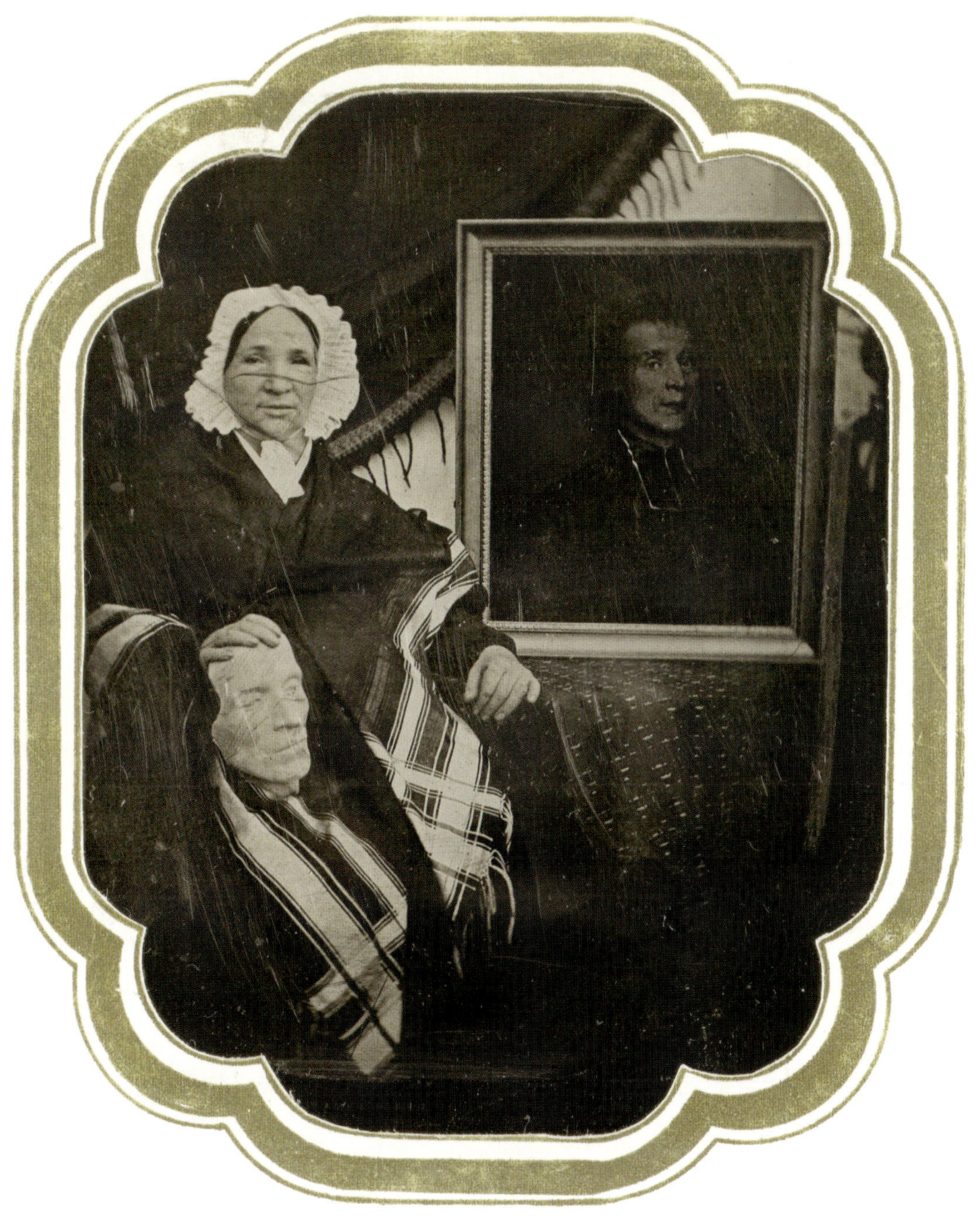

▷ 9   Barthélemy Thalamas   Metaphorical Portrait, Toulouse
Ca. 1850, daguerreotype, Musée d'Orsay, Paris

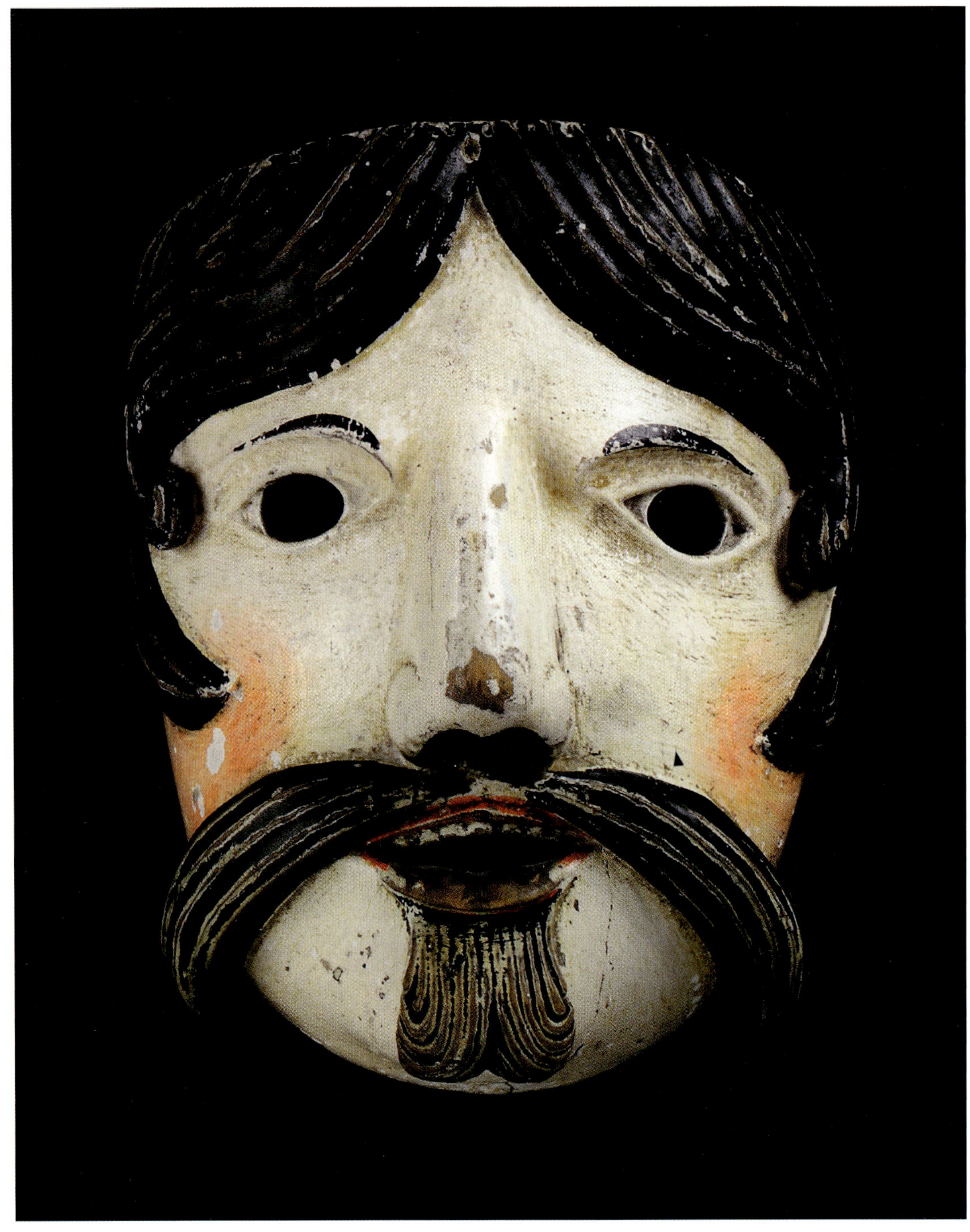

▷ 10   Germany (Oberelsbach)   Carnival's Mask (Face of a Man)
Ca. 1850–60, lime wood, painted in color, Rhönmuseum, Fladungen

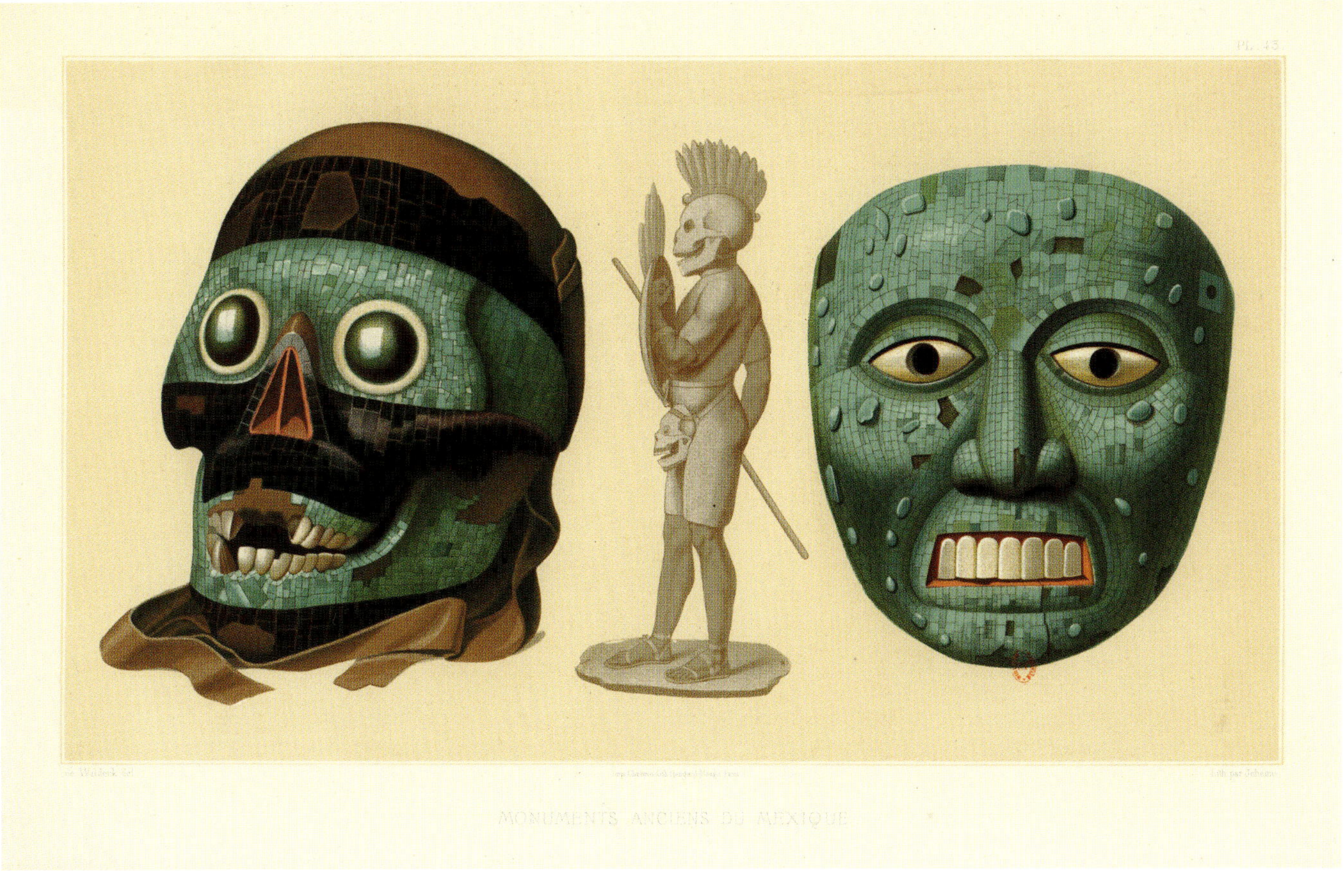

17

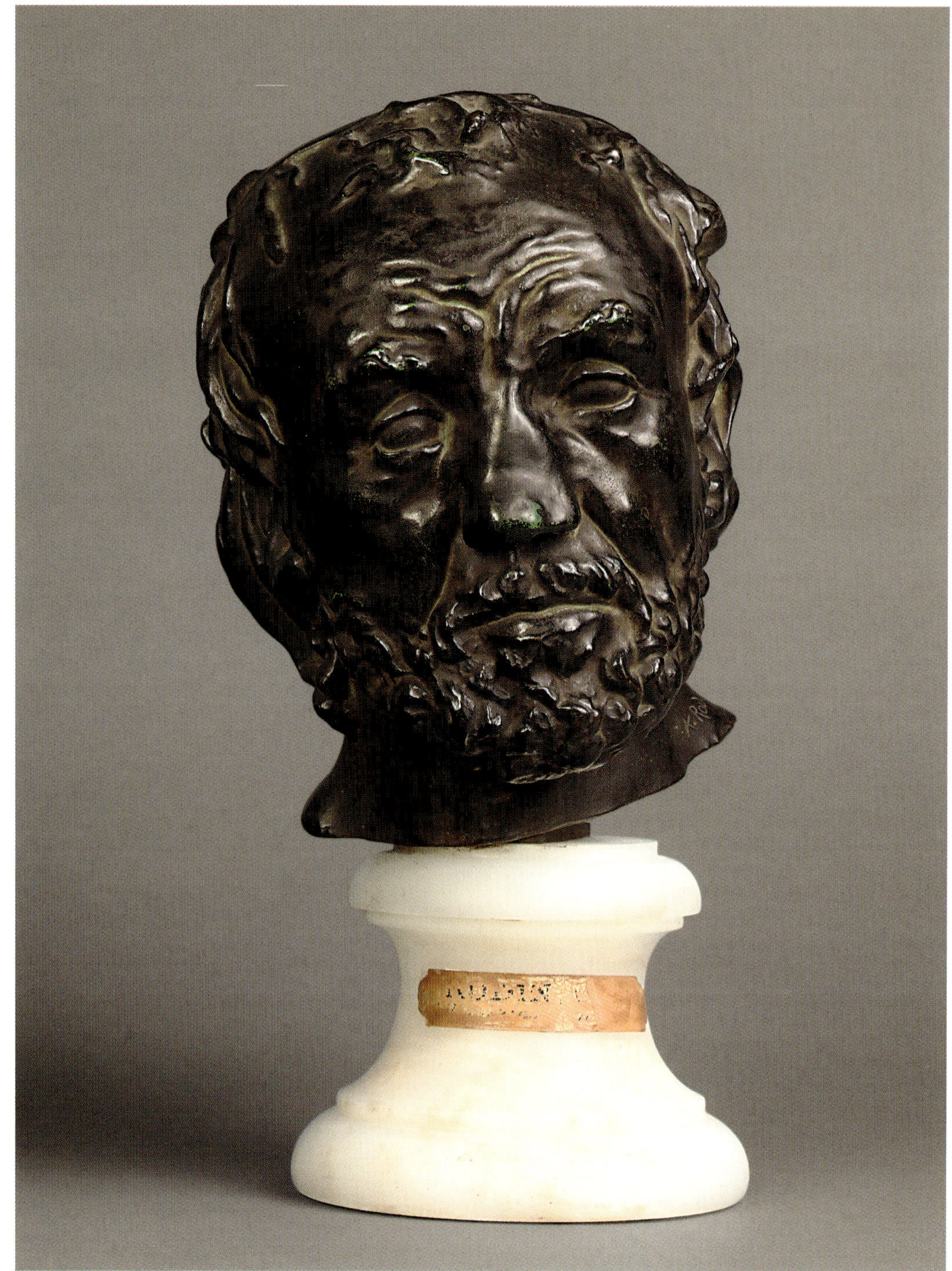

 ▷ 12 **Auguste Rodin** Man with Broken Nose Between 1862 and 1864, bronze, Musée d'Orsay, Paris

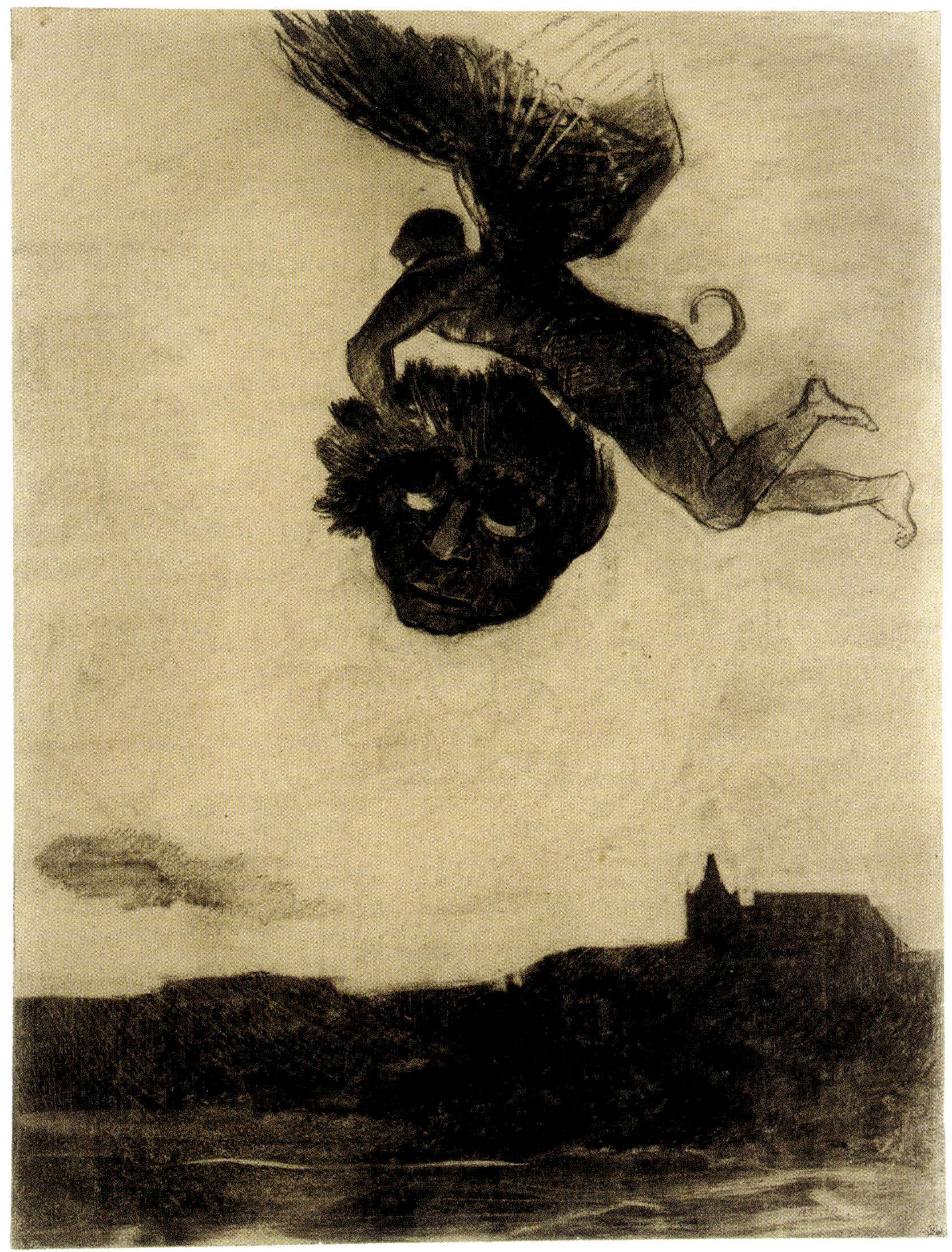

▷ 13   Odilon Redon   Devil, Carrying a Head   1876, pencil and coal on paper, Musée d'Orsay, Paris

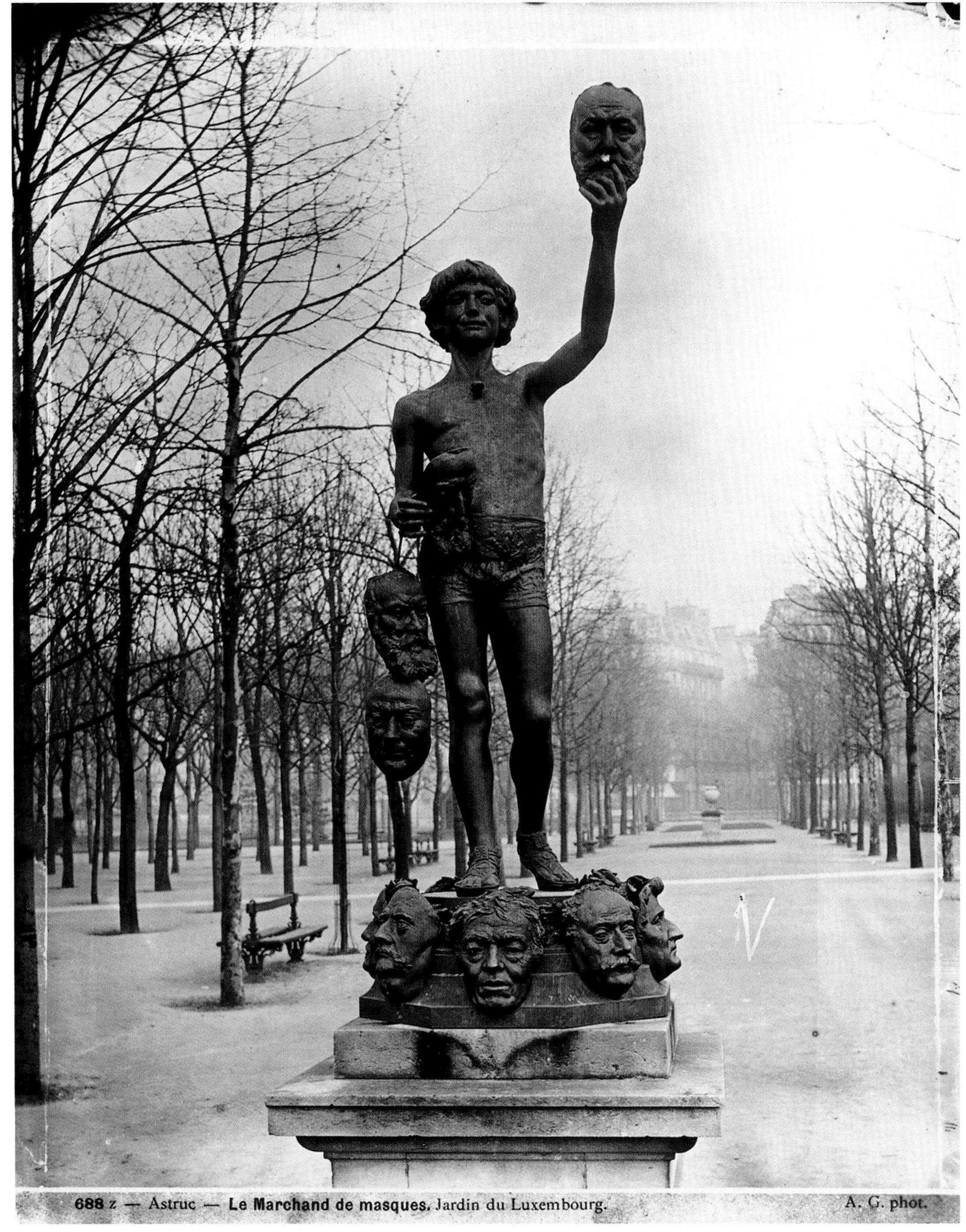

  ▷ 14 **Zacharie Astruc** The Merchant of Masks 1883, bronze, Jardin du Luxembourg, permanent loan Musée d'Orsay, Paris

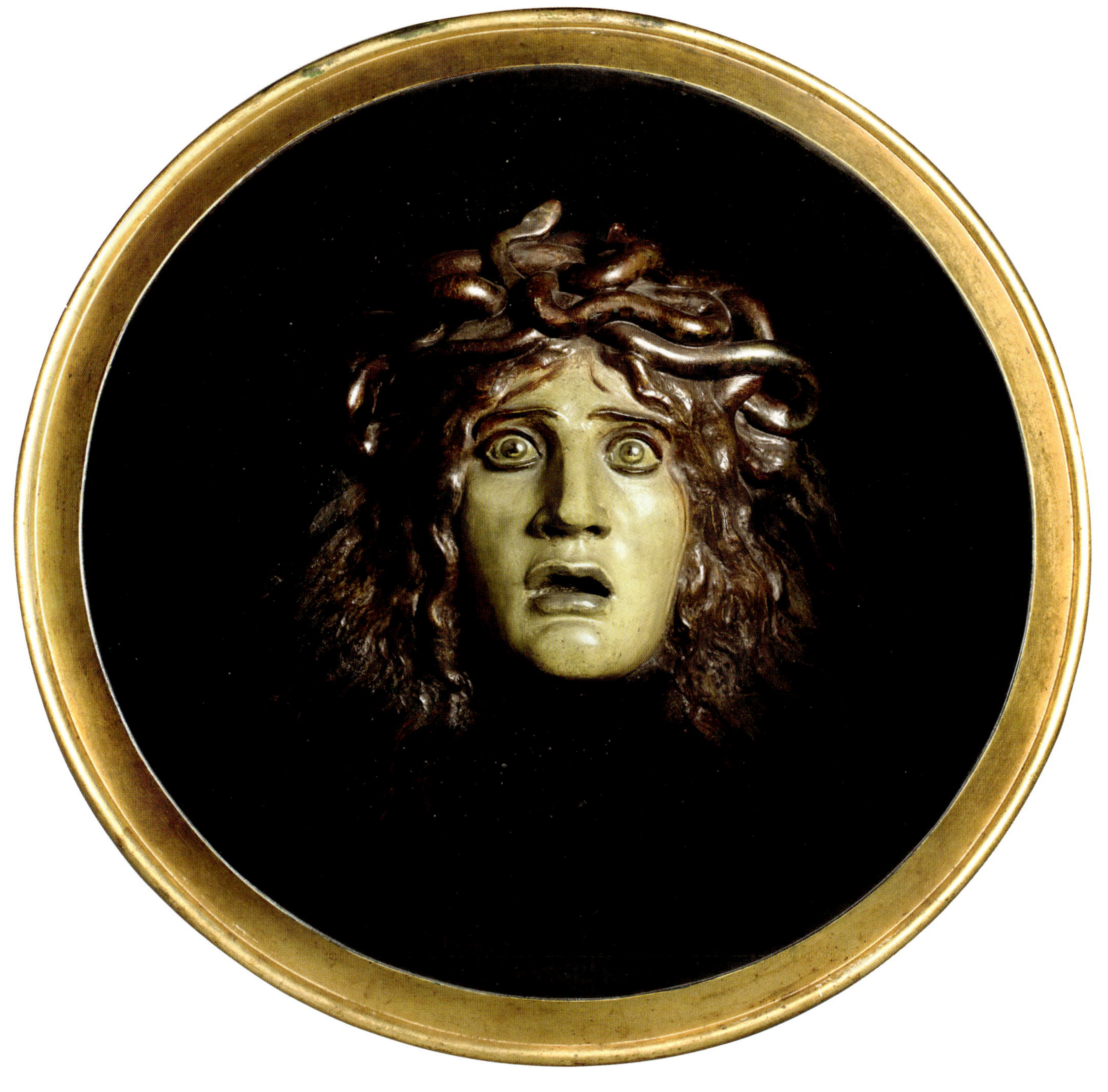

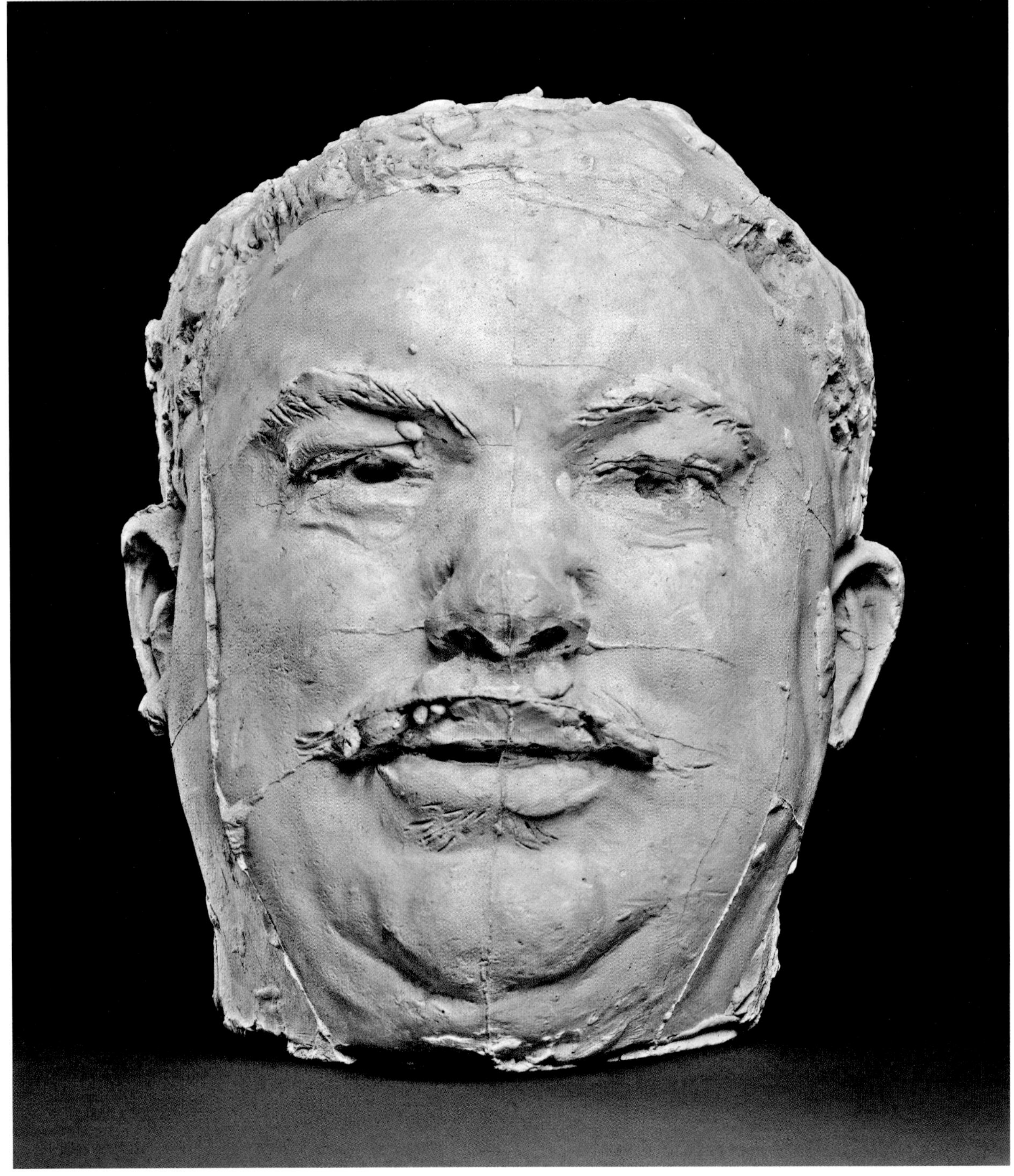

22 ▷ 16 **Auguste Rodin**   Mask of Balzac (also known as Driver of Tours)   1891, plaster, Musée Rodin, Paris

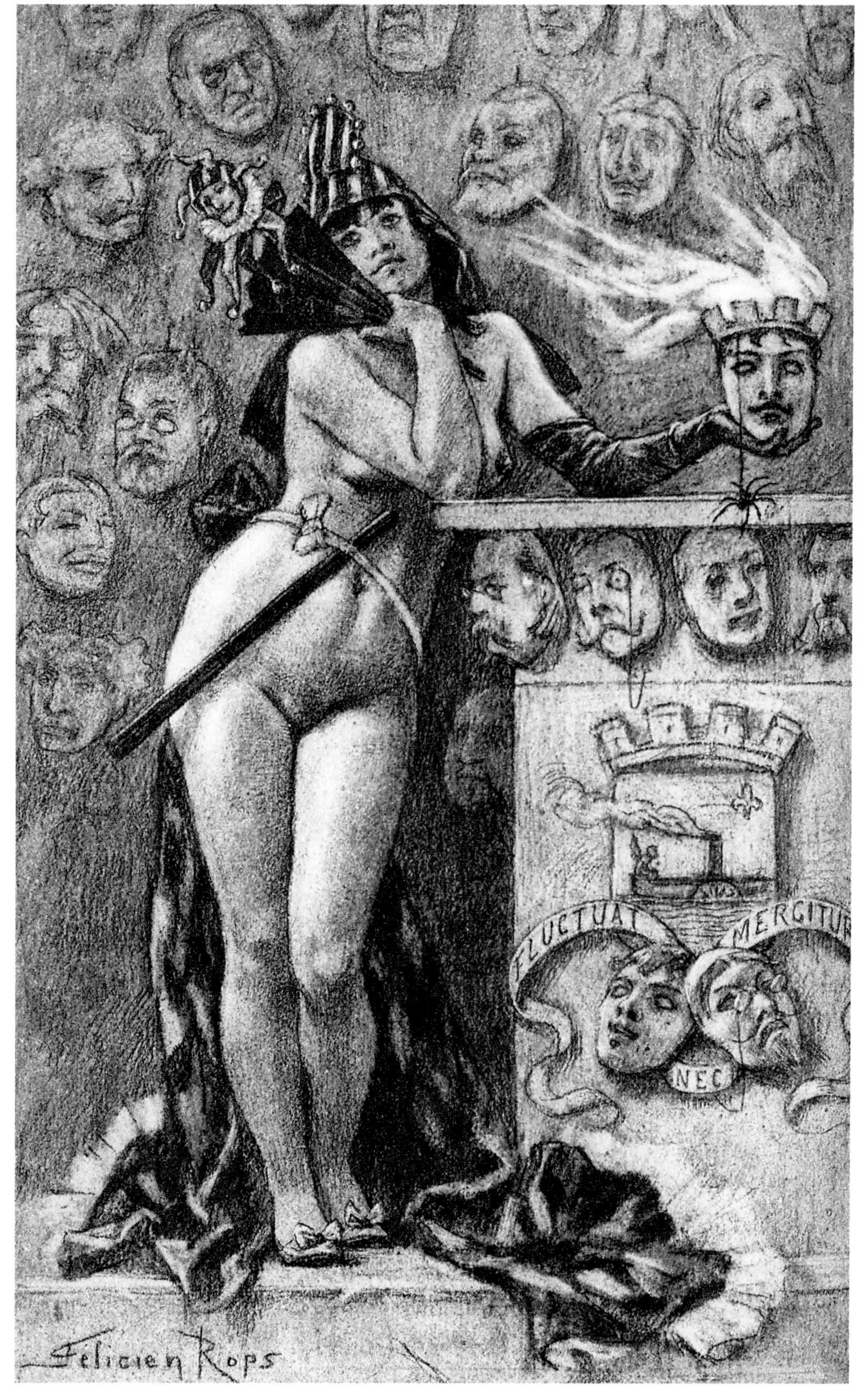

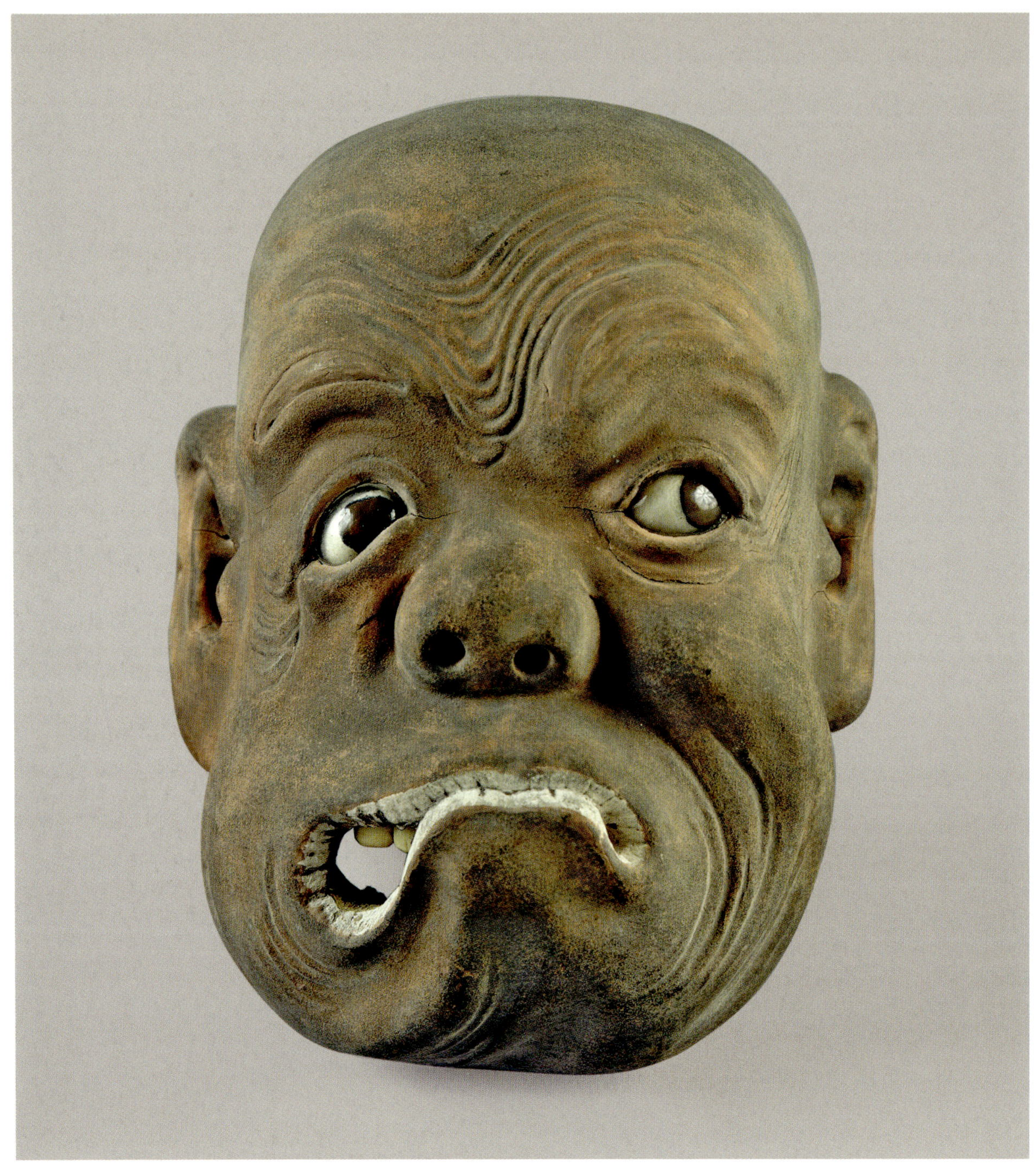

▷ 18   **Unknown artist (Japan)**   Mask (Face Distorted by Grimace)
Nineteenth century, wood, painted in color, glass, Musée Rodin, Paris

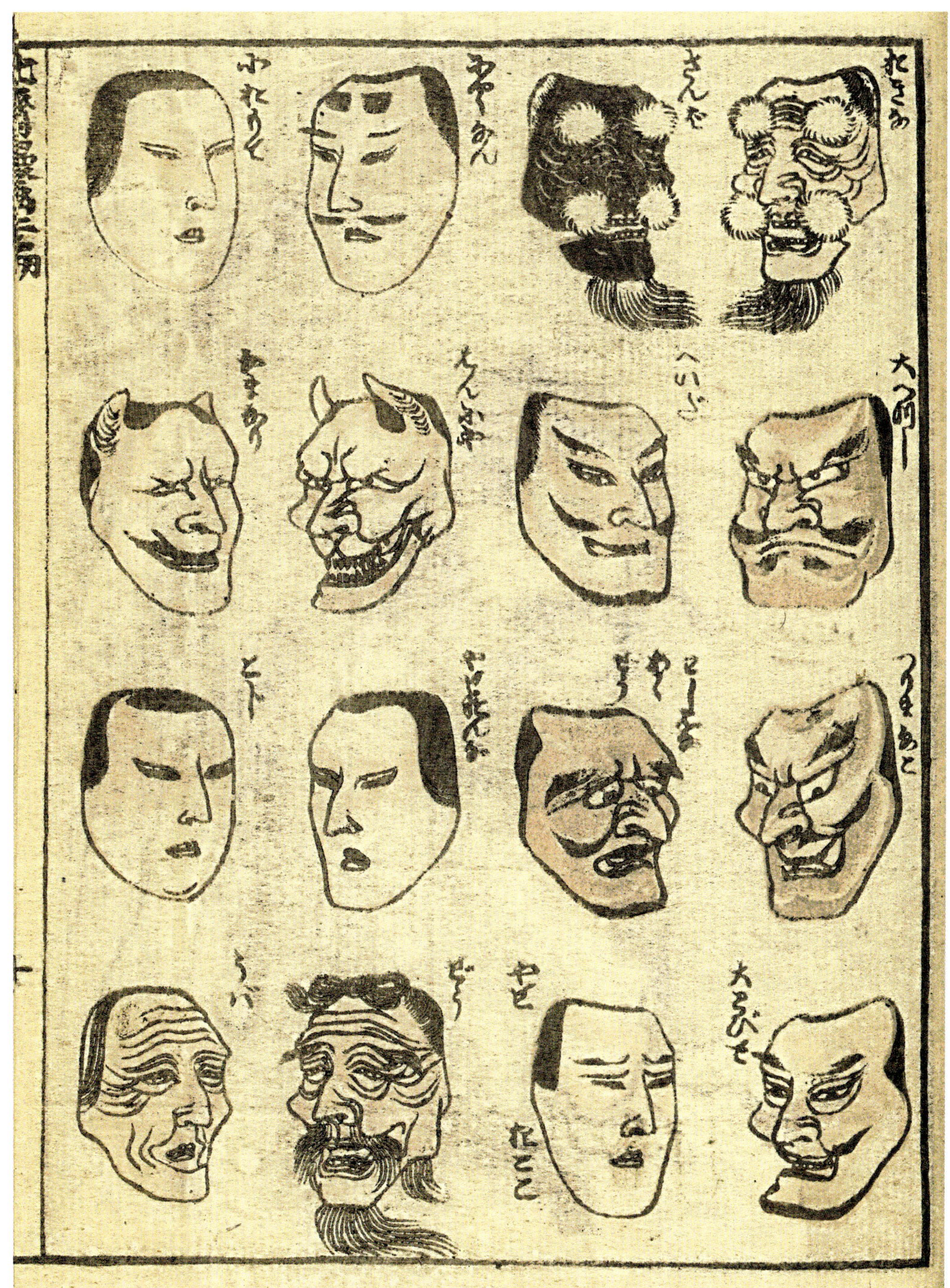

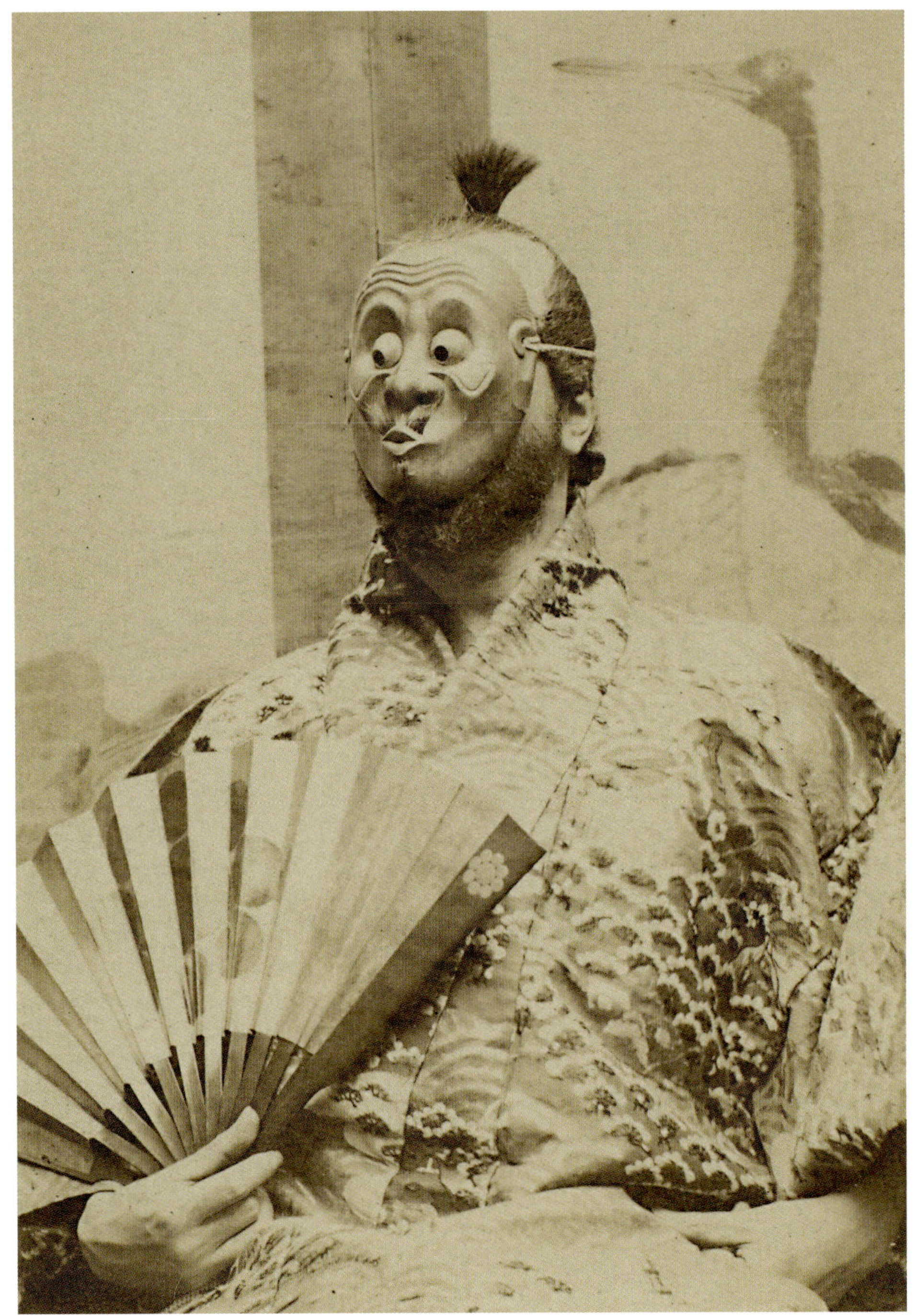

▷ 18 **Unknown photographer (France)** Louis Gonse Dressed up with Japanese Mask
Ca. 1890, photograph, private collection, Lille

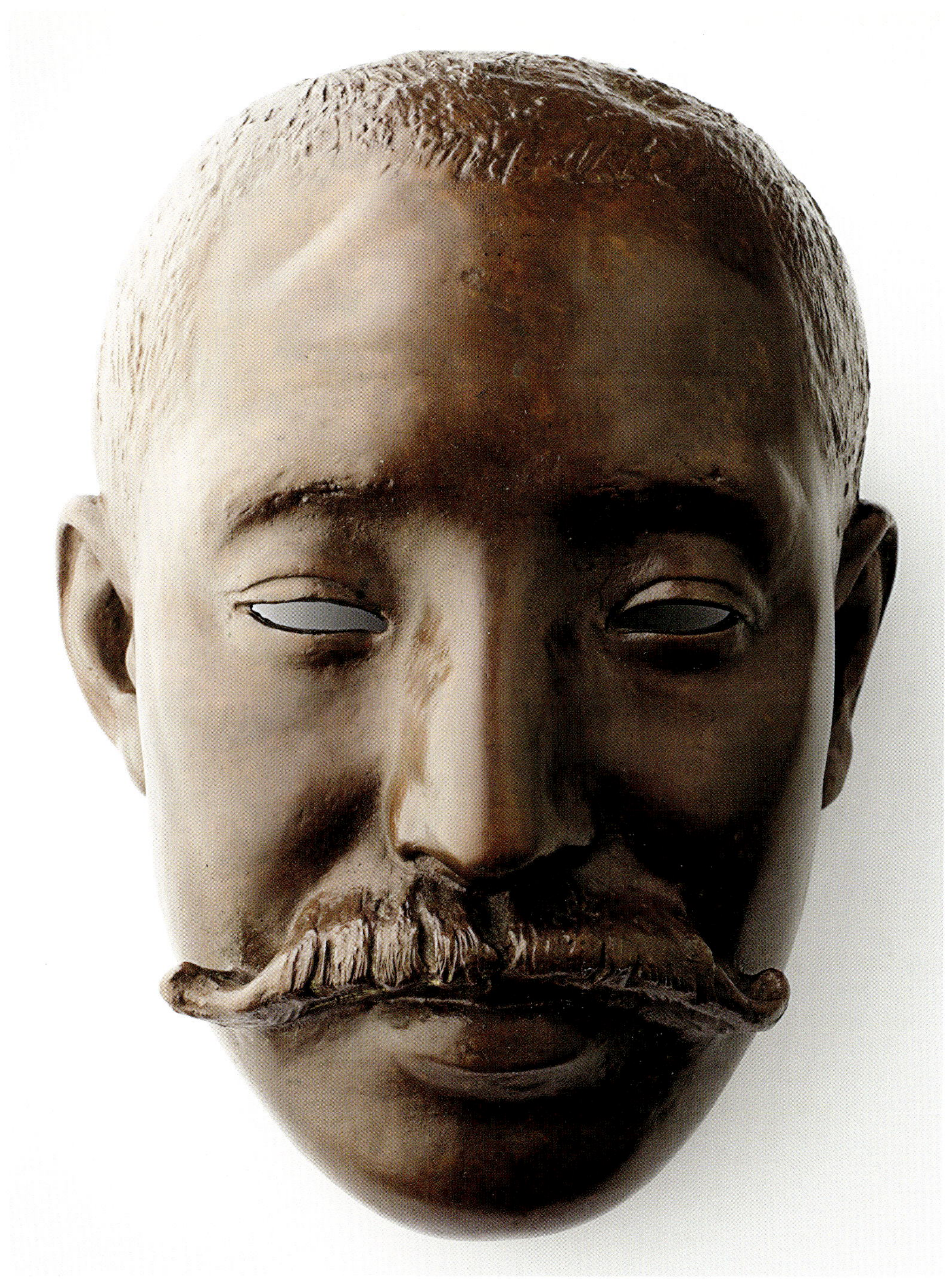

▷ 18   Albert Batholomé   **Mask of Tadamasa Hayashi**
1892, bronze, Musée d'Orsay, Paris

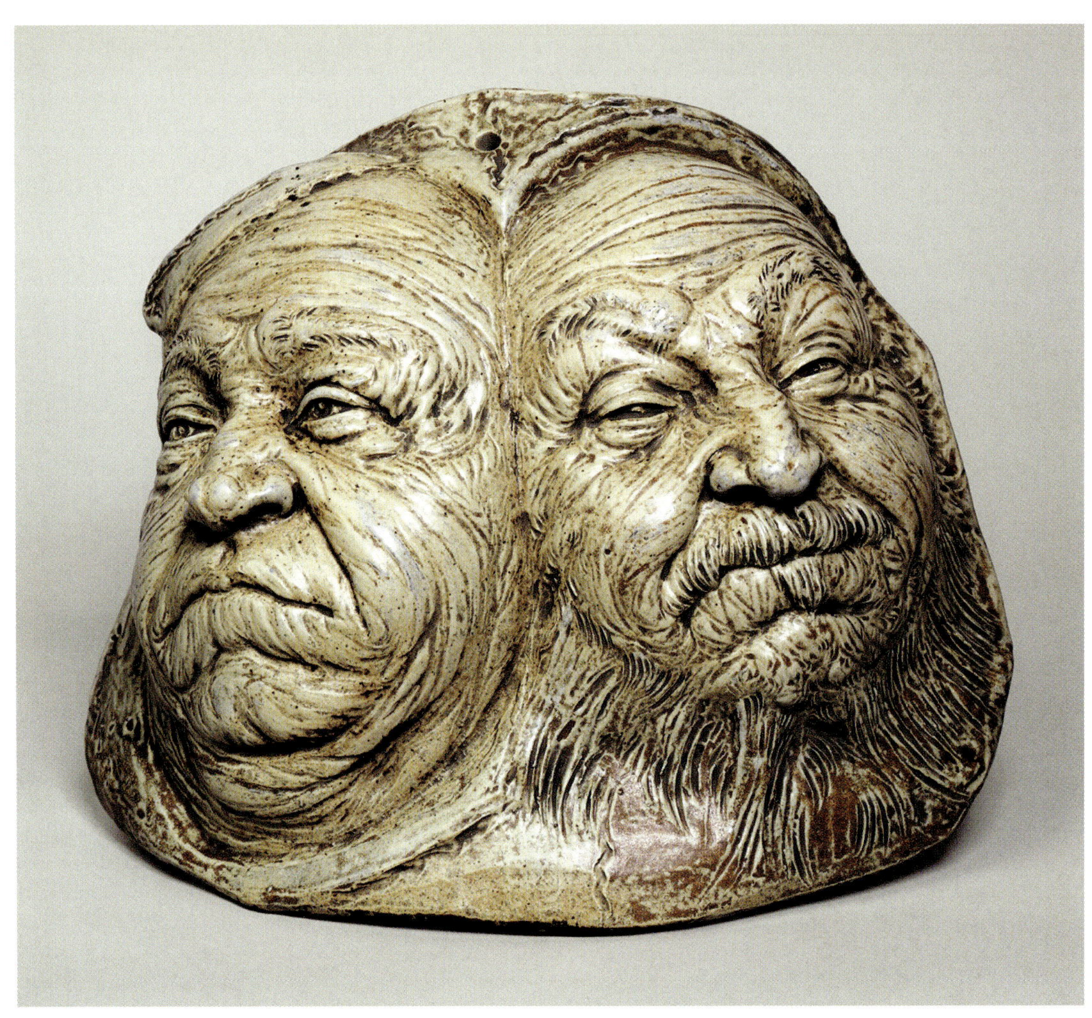

▷ 19   **Jean-Joseph Carriès**   Double Mask

1891, earthenware, glazed, Petit Palais, Musée des Beaux-Arts de la Ville de Paris

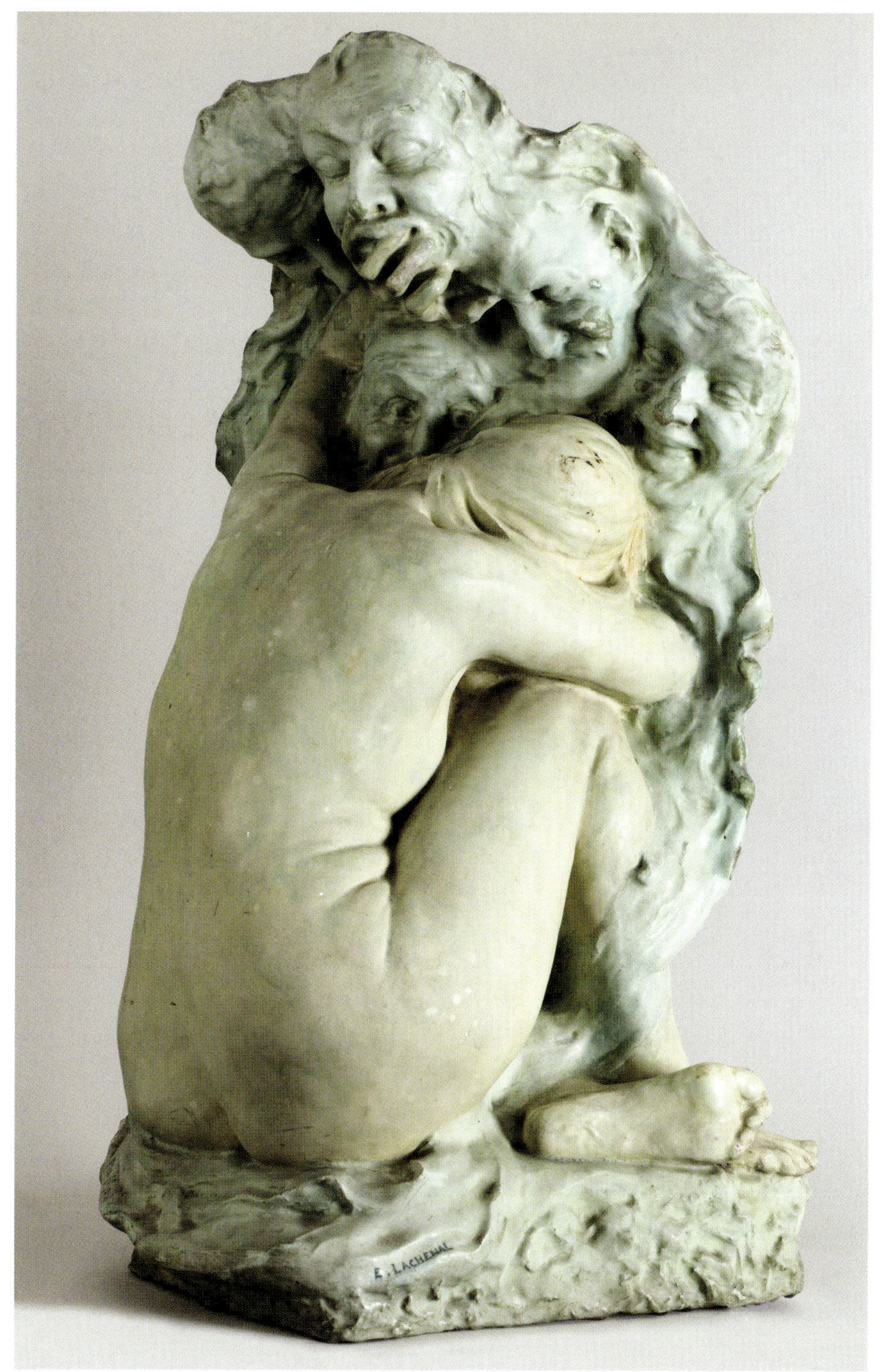

▷ 20 Pierre Félix Masseau (known professionally as Fix-Masseau) The Occupation
1895, earthenware, glazed, private collection, Compiègne   29

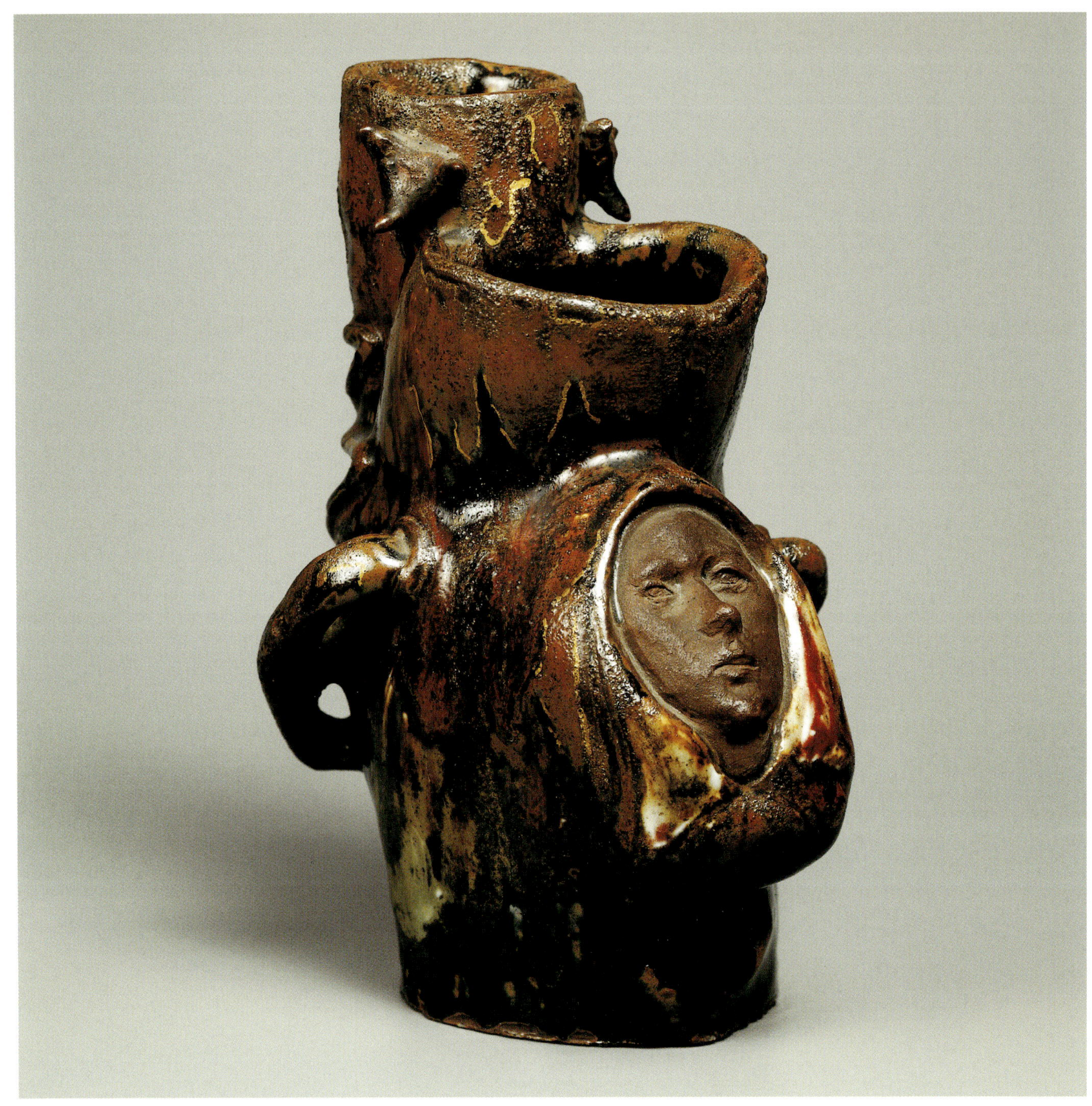

▷ 21   Paul Gauguin   Double Vase with Woman's Mask
1887/88, earthenware, partly glazed, Ny Carlsberg Glyptotek, Copenhagen

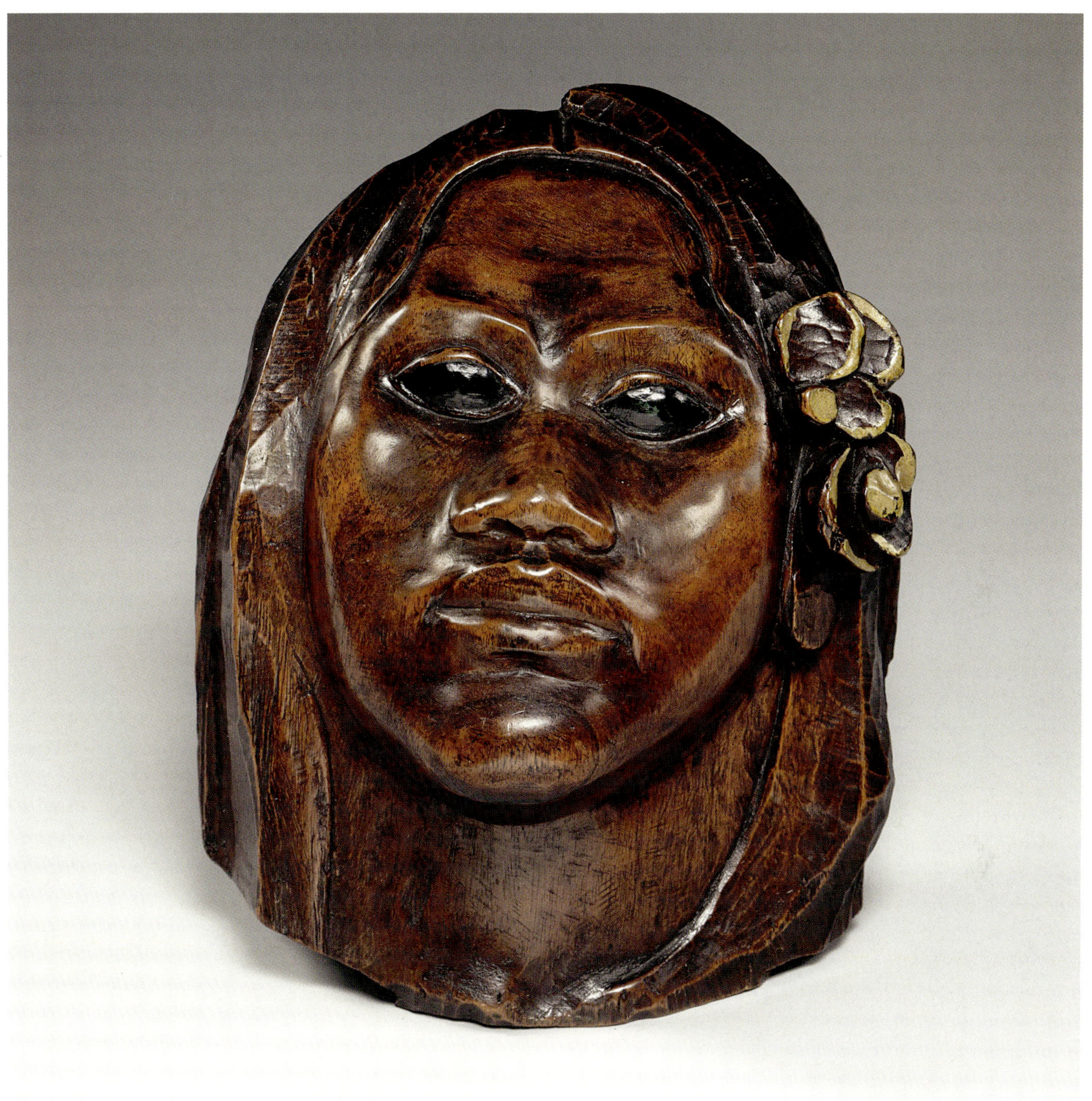

▷ 21 Paul Gauguin Tehura

1891–93, pua wood, painted, Musée d'Orsay, Paris

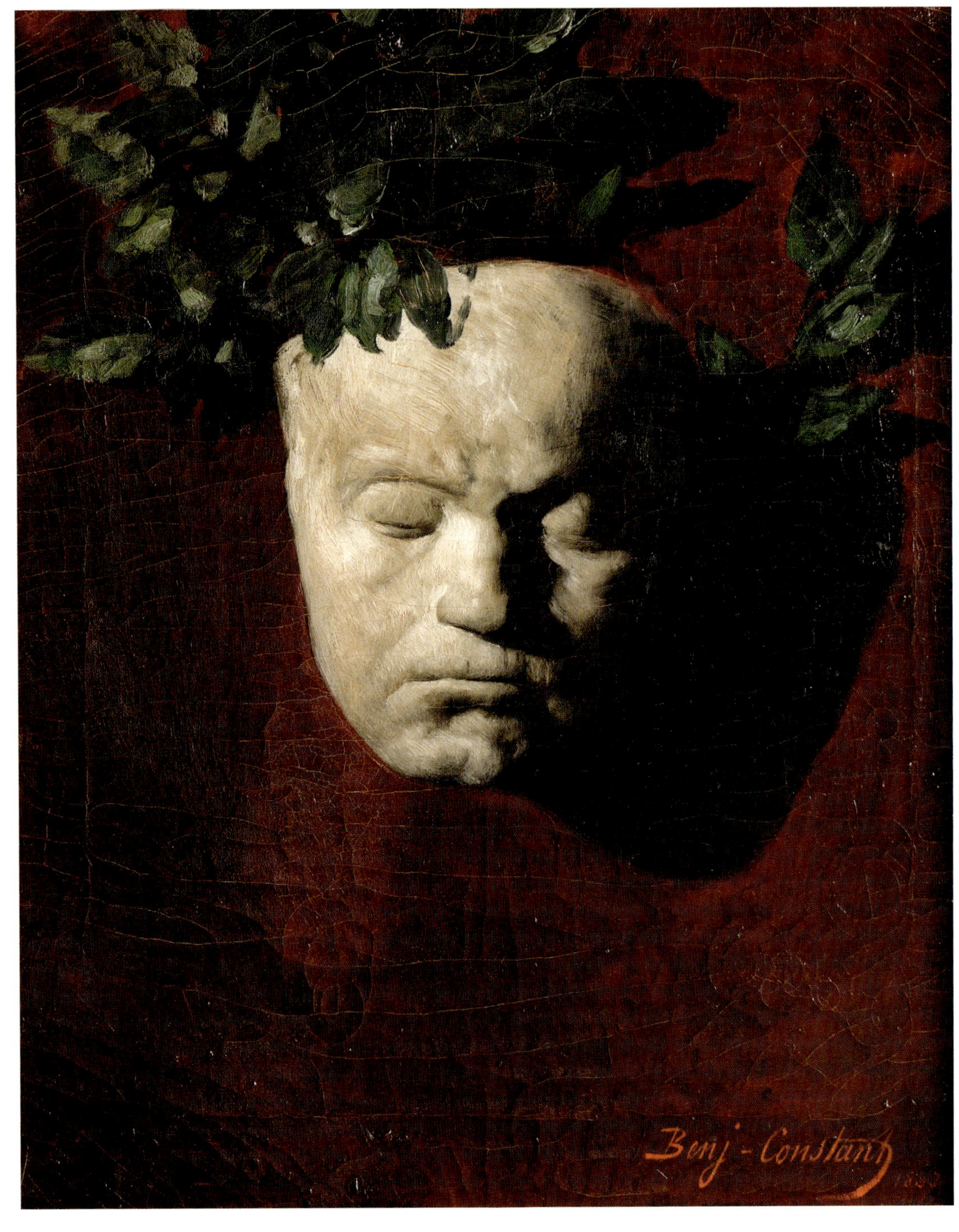

▷ 22   Jean Joseph Constant (known professionally as Benjamin-Constant) **Ludwig van Beethoven's Mask**
Second half of nineteenth century, oil on canvas,
private collection

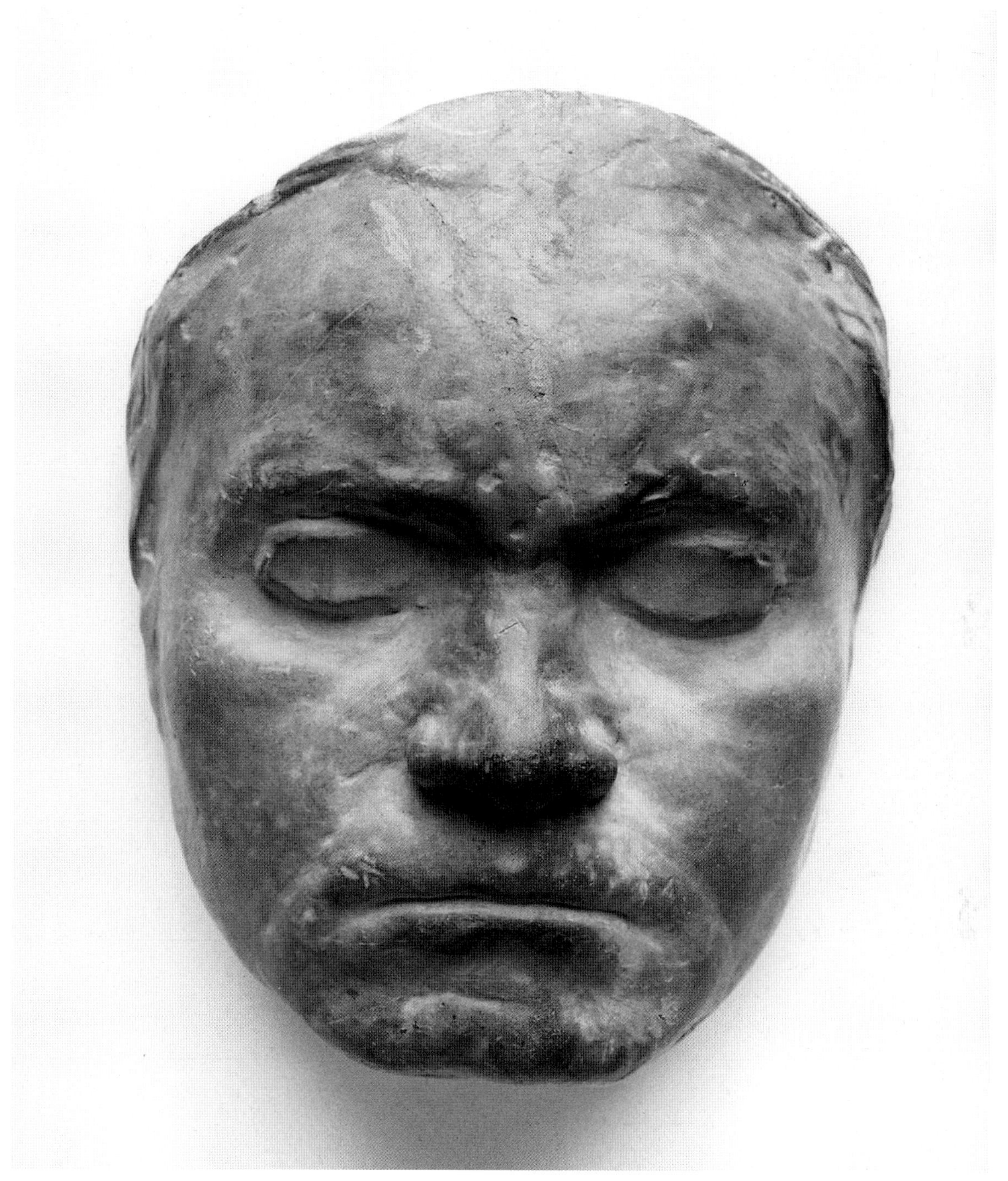

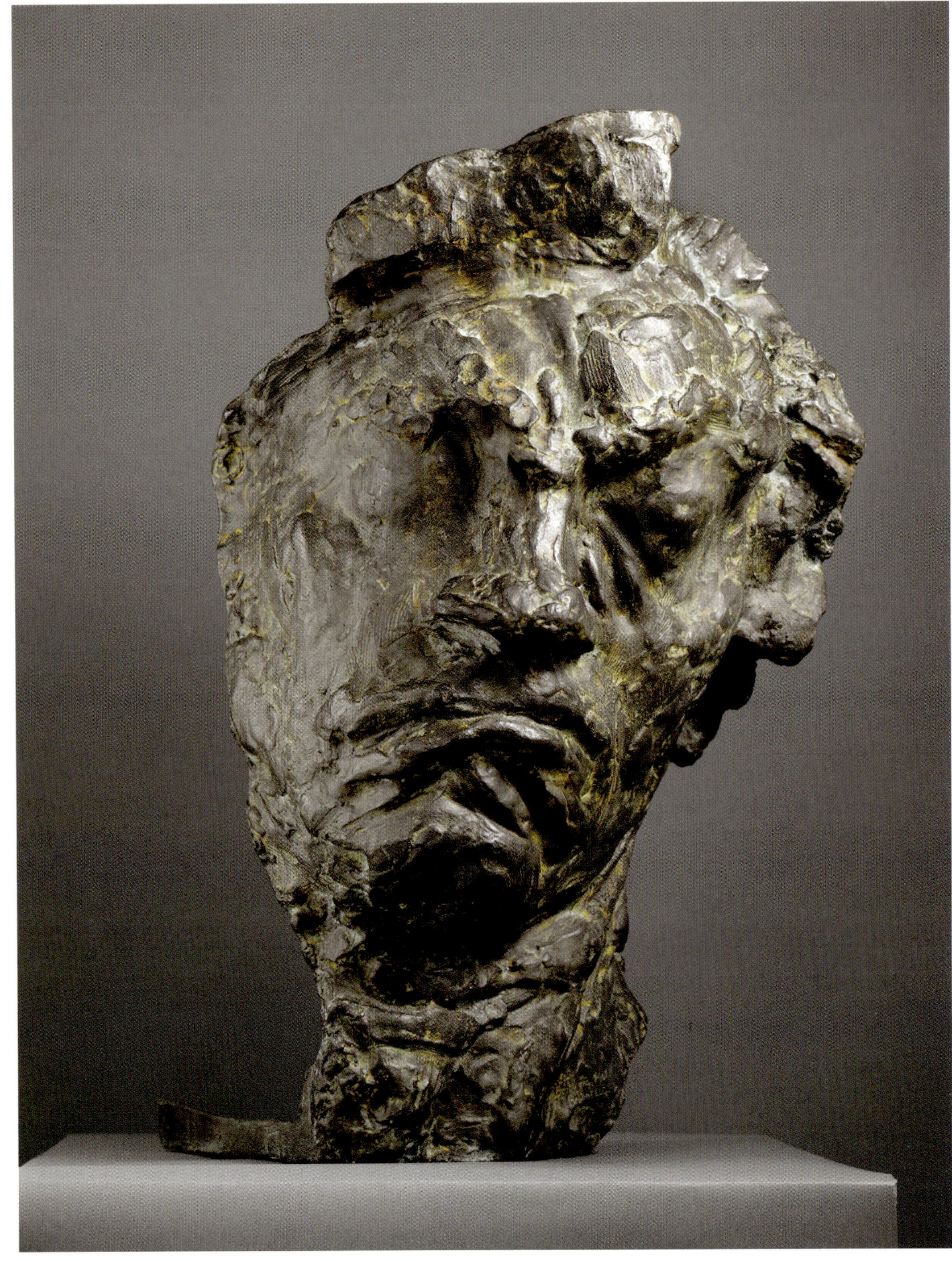

34 ▷ 22 **Antoine Bourdelle** **Beethoven, Great Tragic Mask** 1901, bronze, Musée Bourdelle, Paris

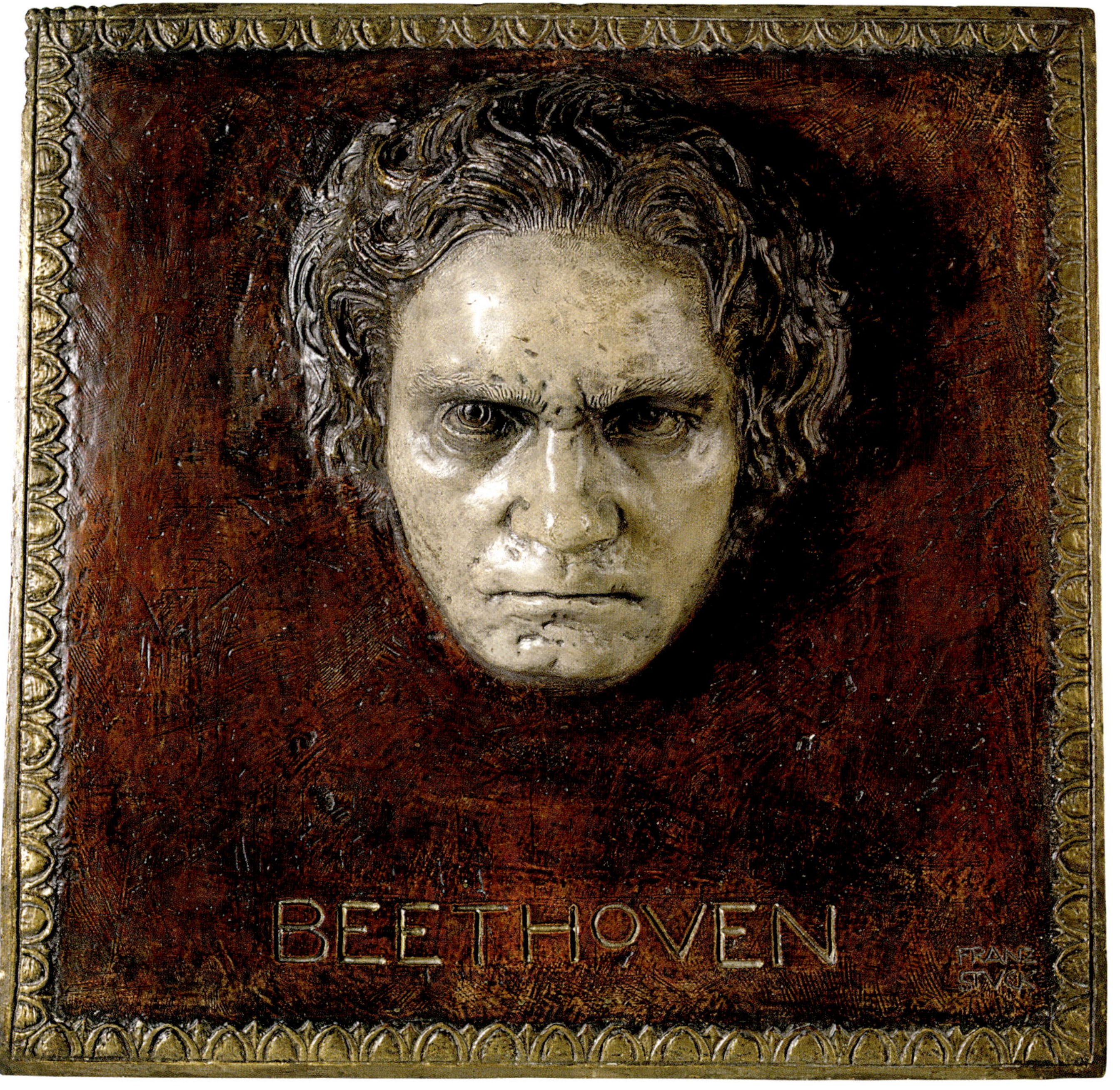

▷ 22   Franz von Stuck   Ludwig van Beethoven   1902, plaster, painted and gold-plated, Musée d'Orsay, Paris   35

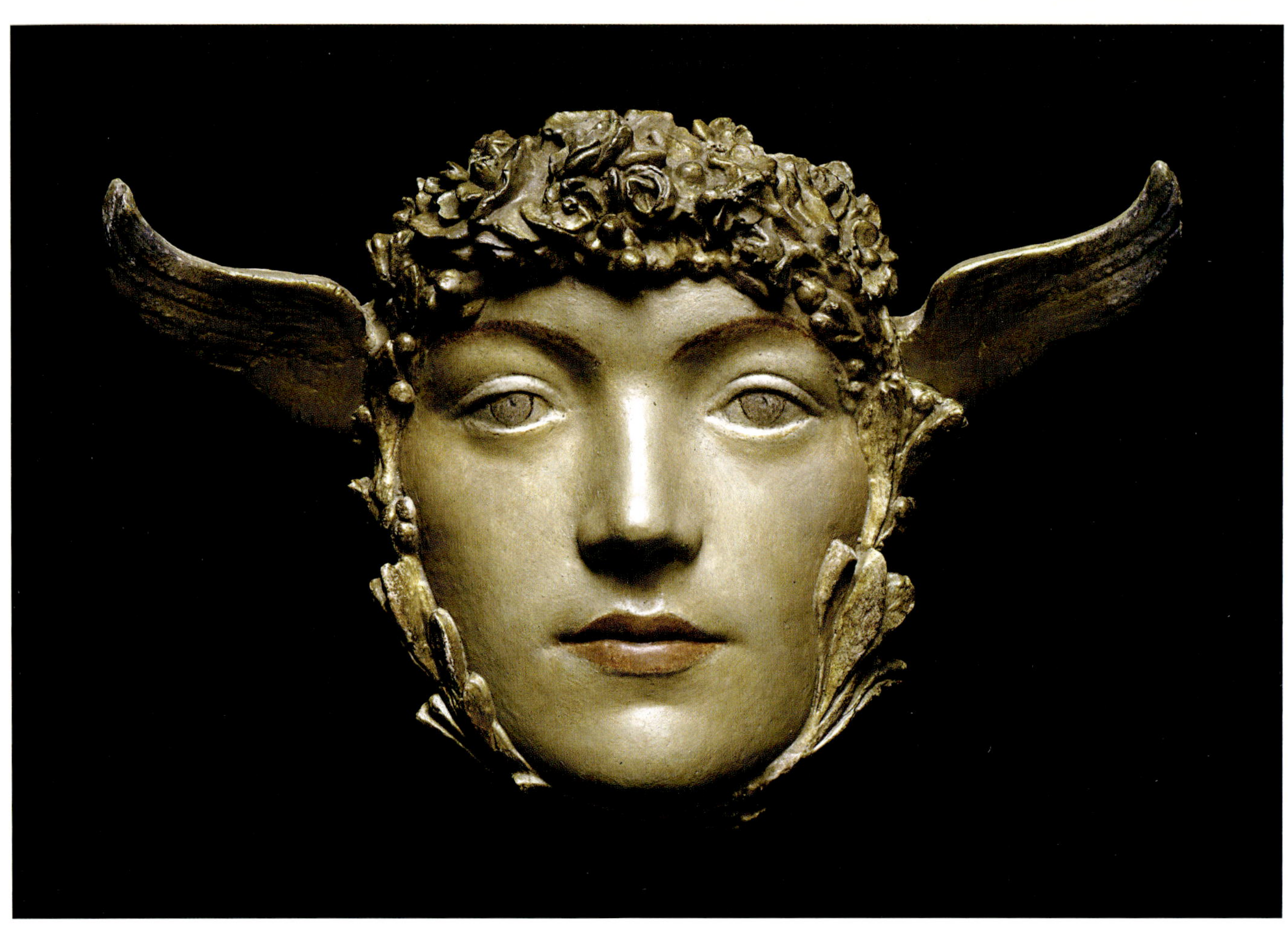

  ▷ 23 **Fernand Khnopff** **A Mask** Ca. 1897, plaster (gesso duro), painted, Hamburger Kunsthalle, Hamburg

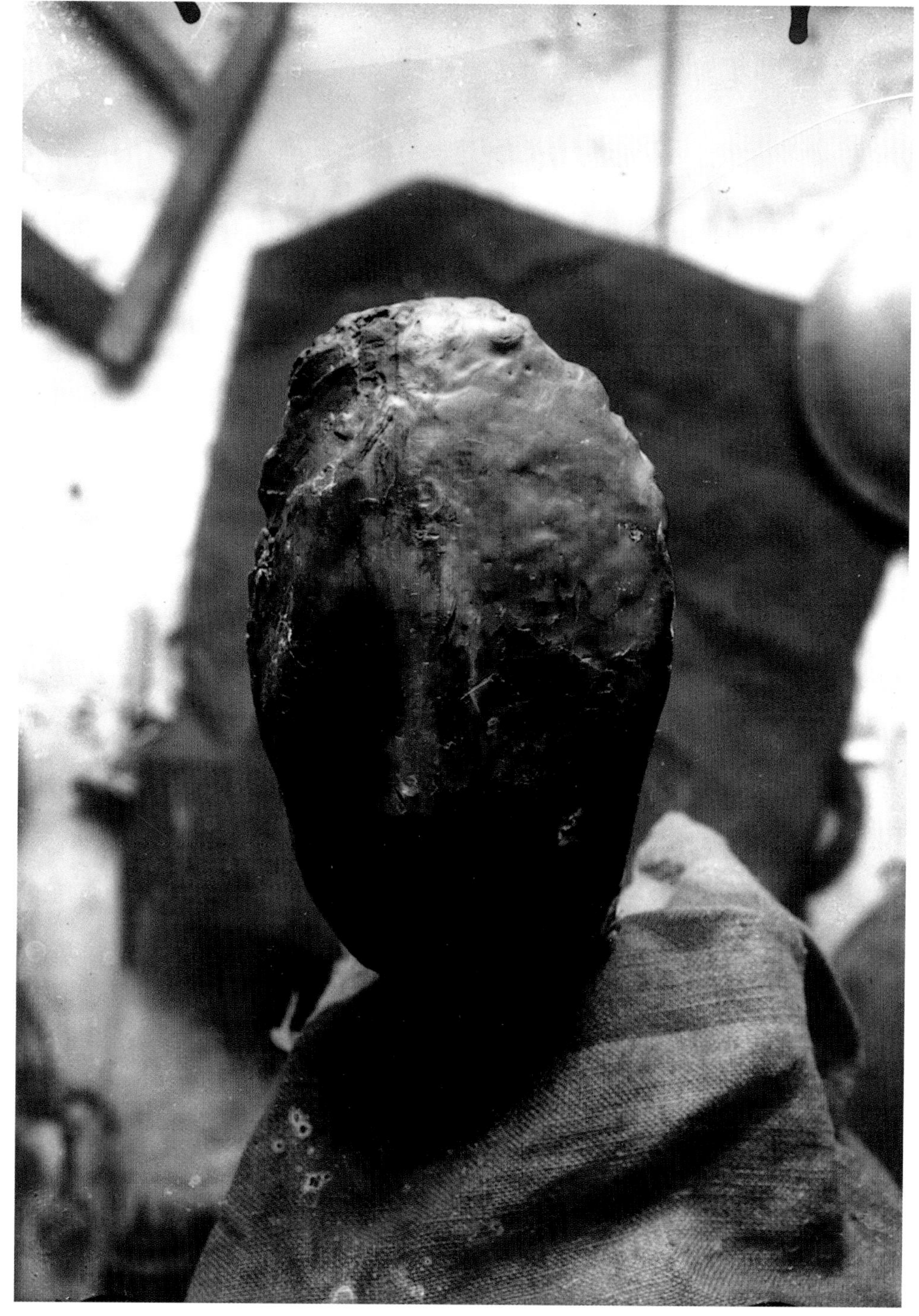

▷ 24 **Medardo Rosso** Madame X 1896, modern copy of a glass negative, Museo Medardo Rosso, Barzio

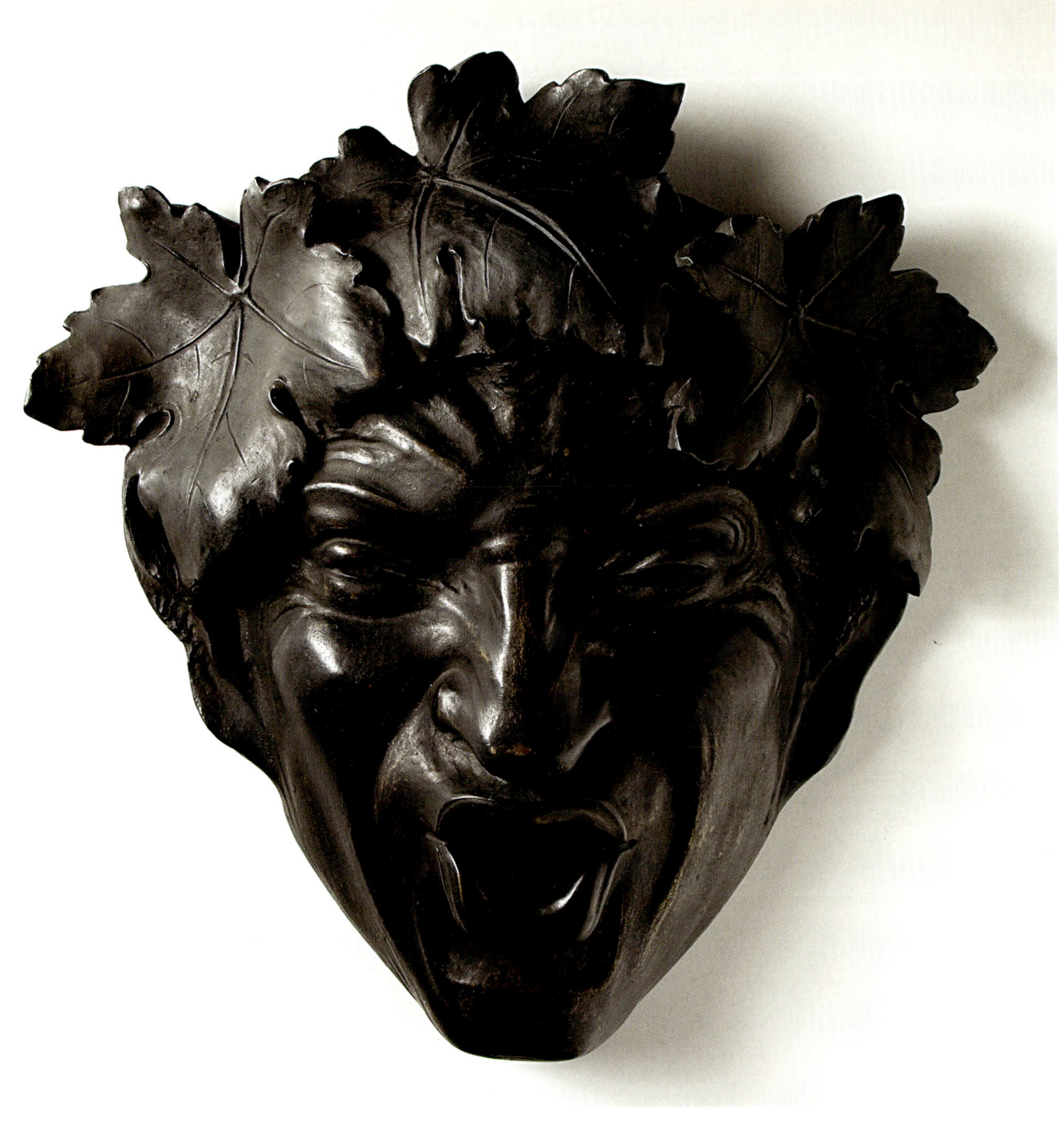

▷ 25   Ludwig Habich   Mask of Bacchus (Waterspout)
1900/01, bronze, Institut Mathildenhöhe Darmstadt,
permanent loan Hessisches Landesmuseum Darmstadt

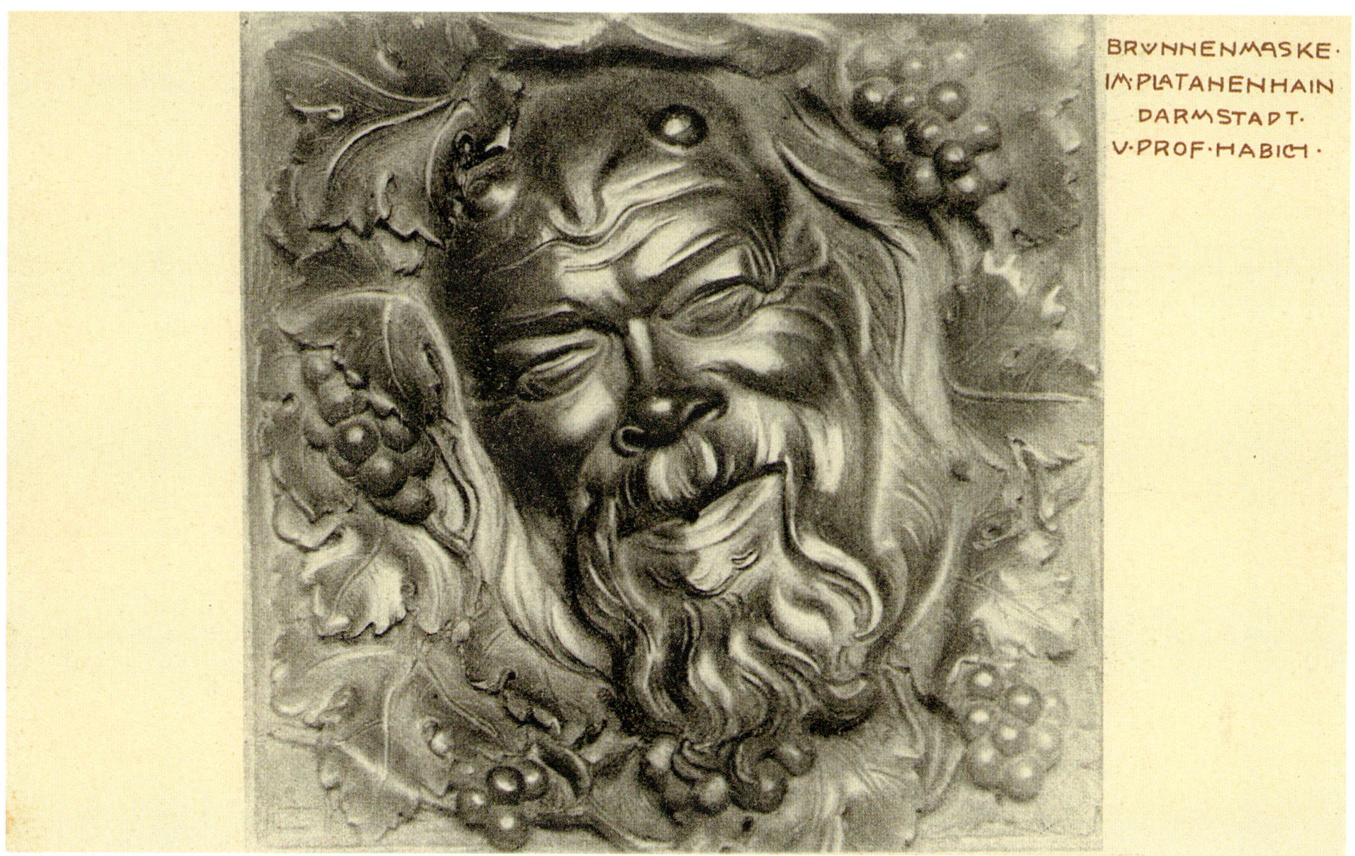

▷ 25   **Ludwig Habich**   Bronze Plate with Bacchus's Head as Waterspout
1901, postcard, Städtische Kunstsammlung, Institut Mathildenhöhe Darmstadt

39

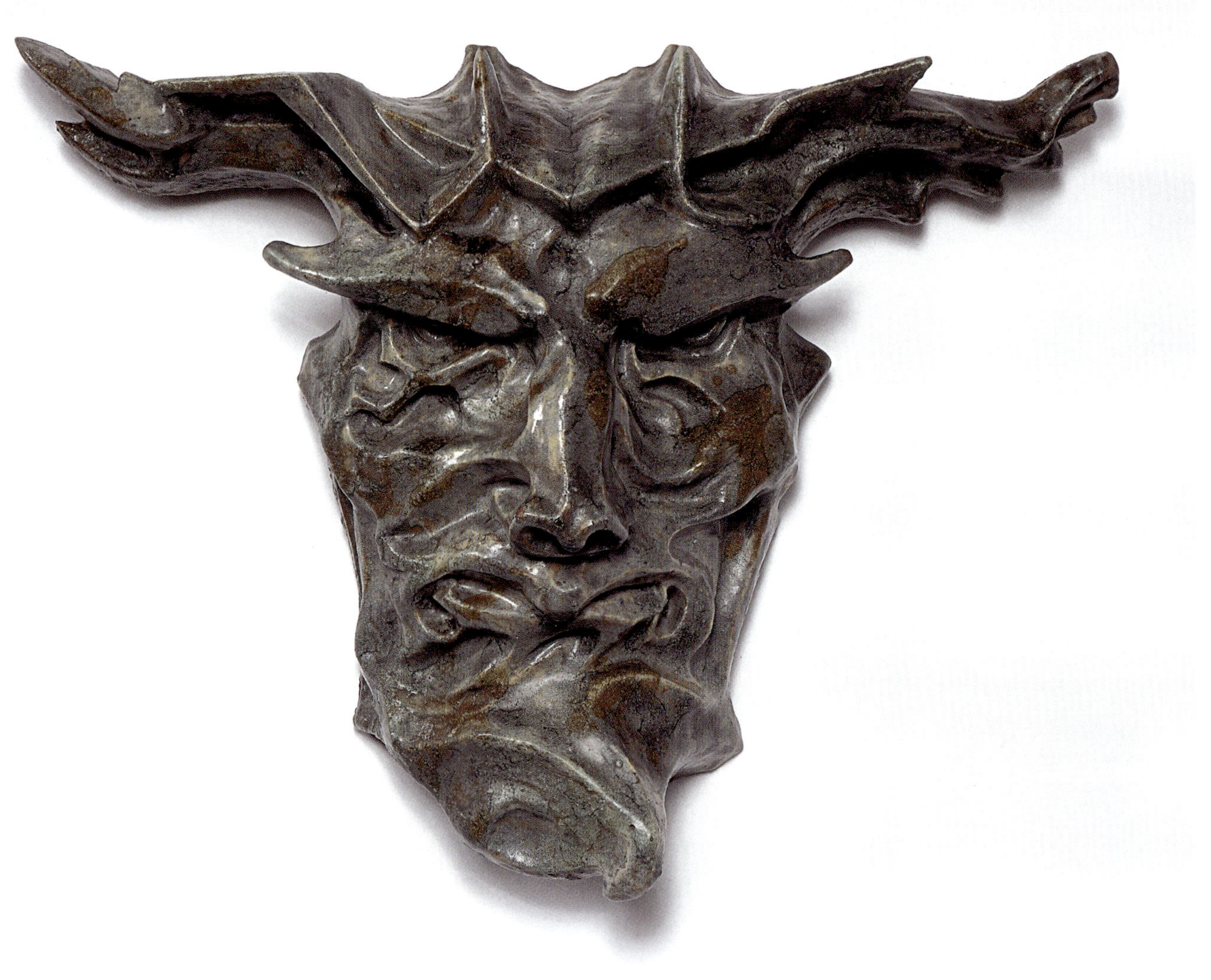

40　▷ 26 **Niels Hansen Jacobsen**　Mask of the Fall　Before 1900, earthenware, glazed, Vejen Kunstmuseum, Vejen

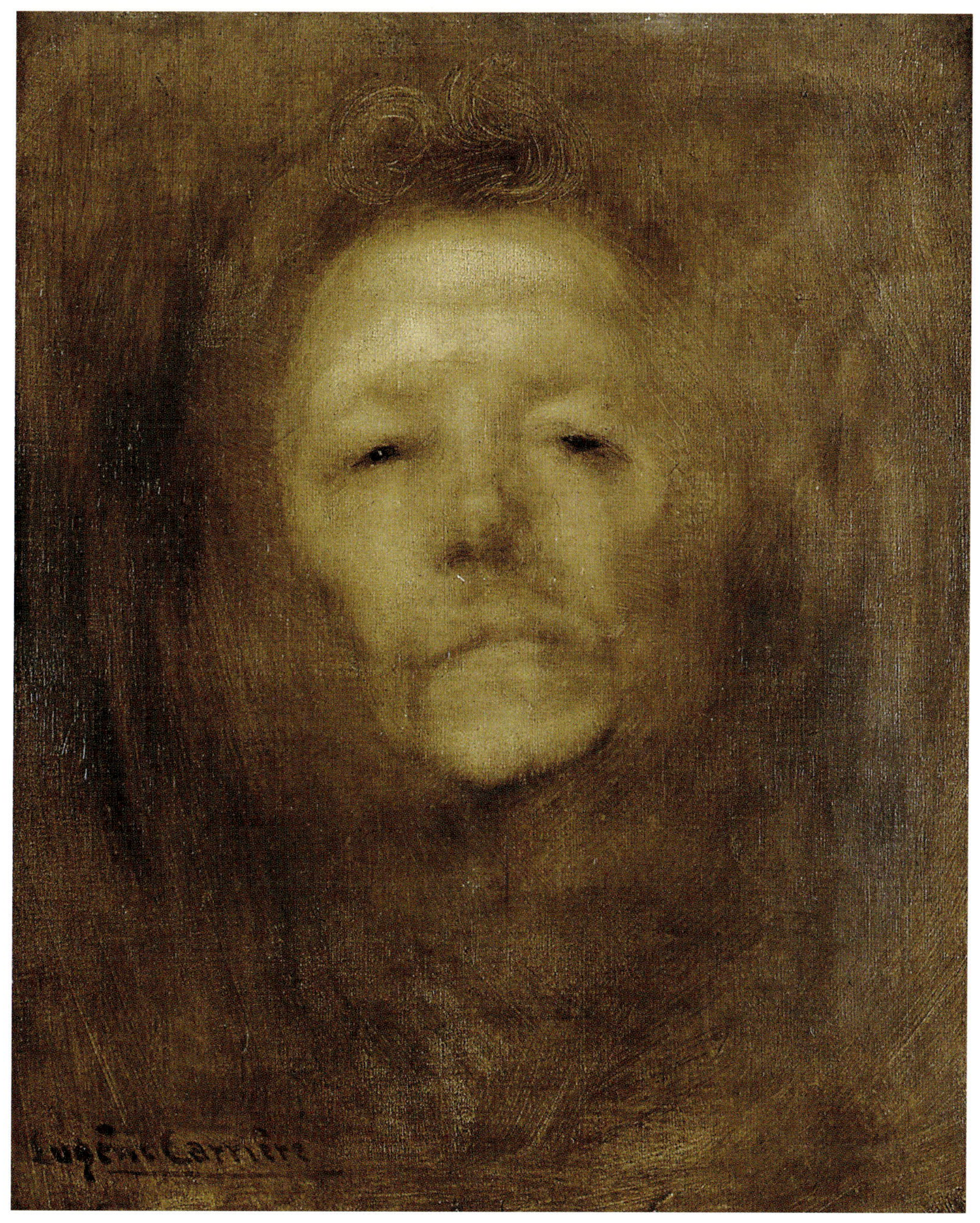

▷ 27 **Eugène Carrière** Self-Portrait 1901, oil on canvas, Musée d'Art Moderne et Contemporain, Strasbourg

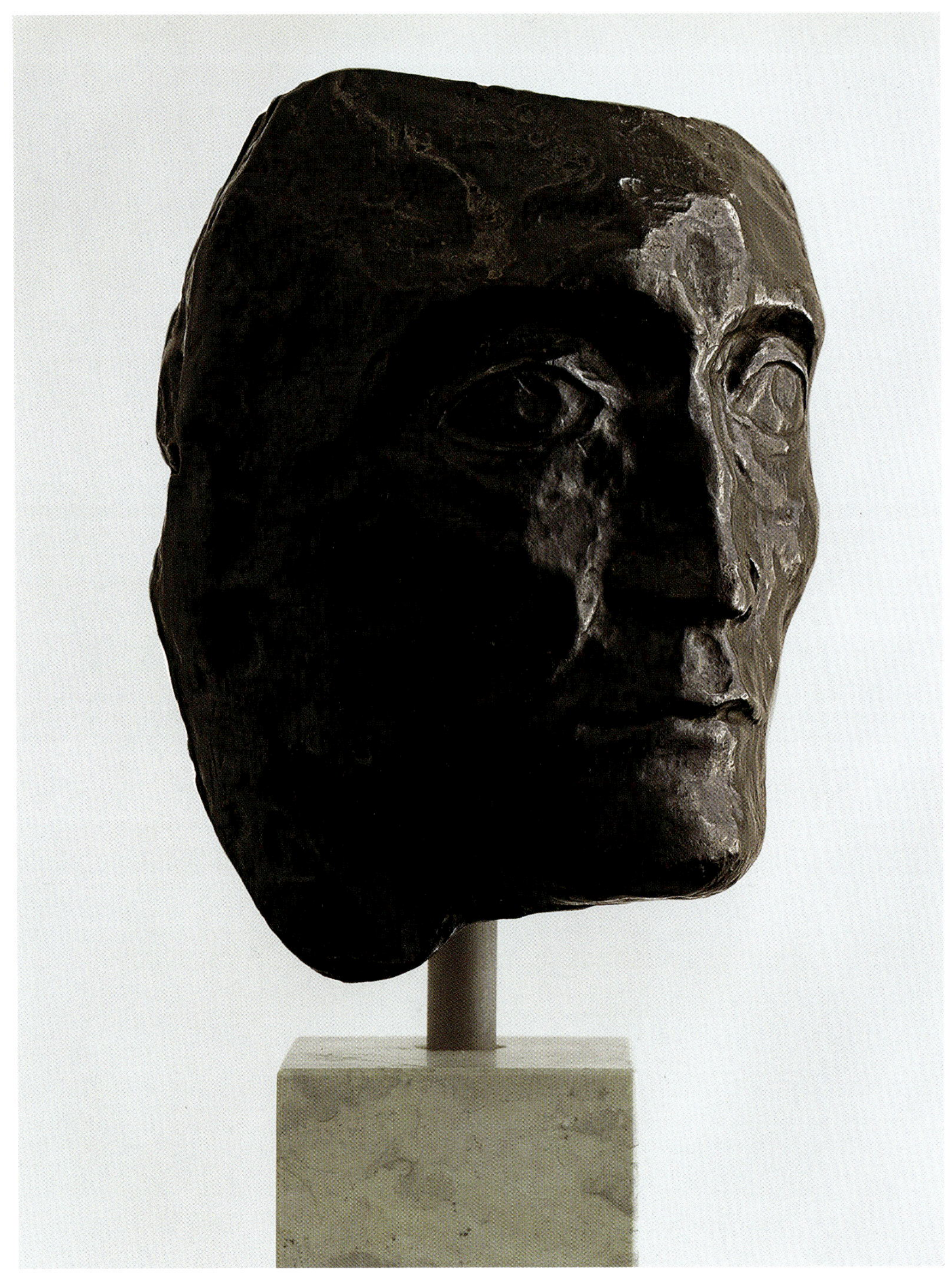

▷ 28   Pablo Picasso   Picador's Mask with Broken Nose
1903, bronze, Kunsthaus Zürich

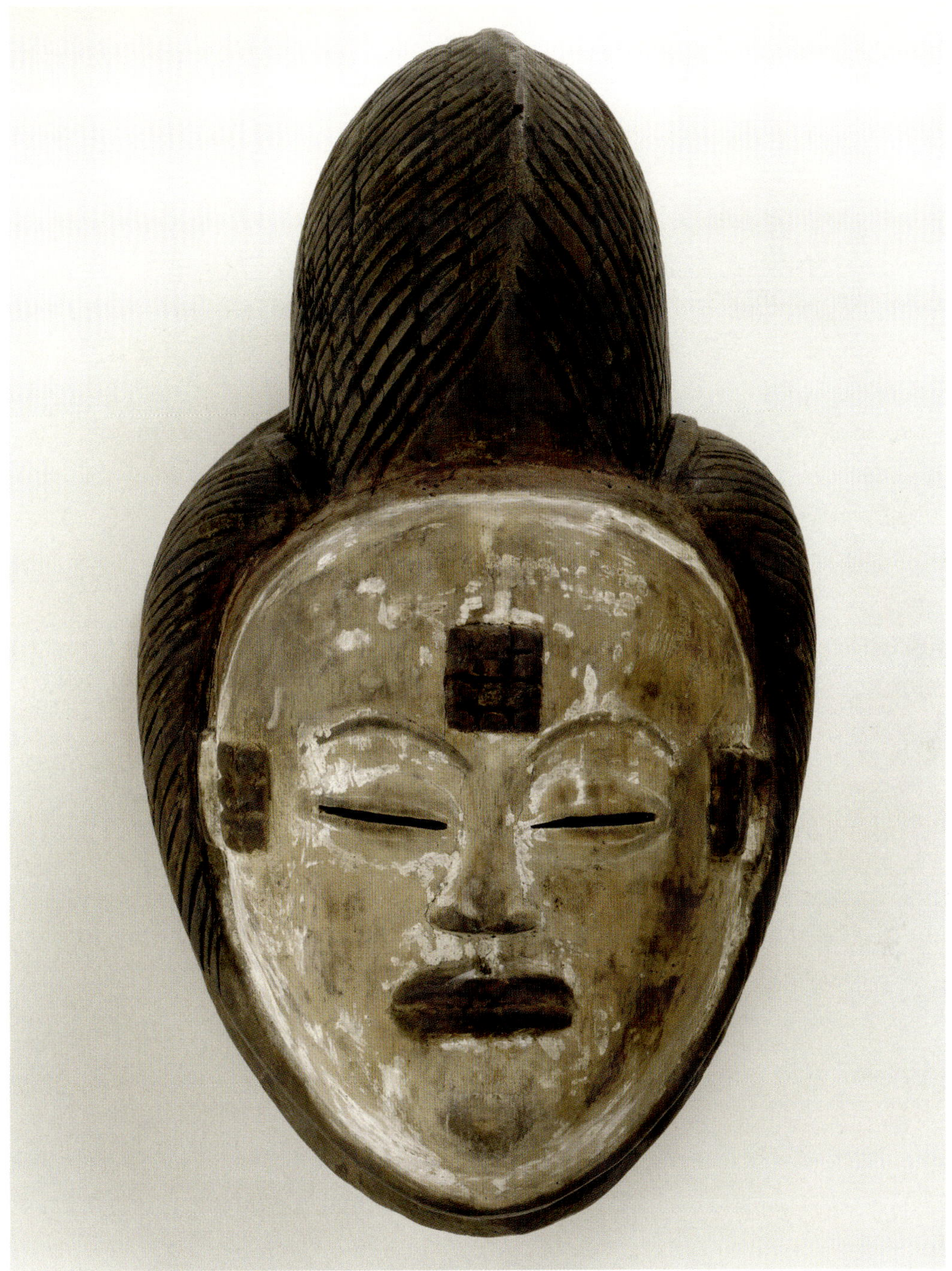

▷ 28   Africa   White Mask of the Beautiful Young Girl Mukuyi
Once owned by Pablo Picasso, nineteenth century, wood, painted, Musée du Quai Branly, Paris

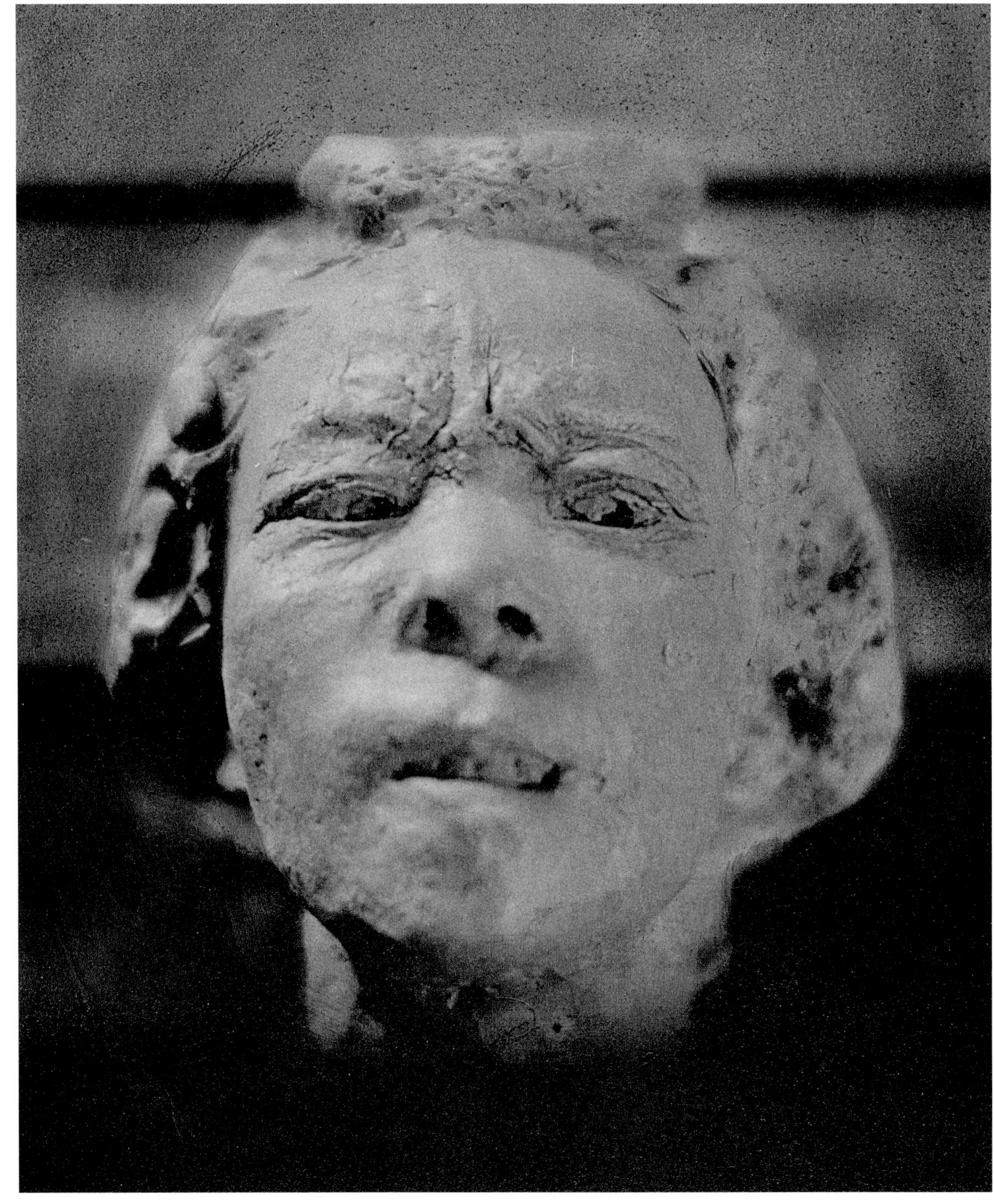

44 ▷ 29 **Edward Steichen** Mask of Hanako Ca. 1908, platinotype, Musée Rodin, Paris

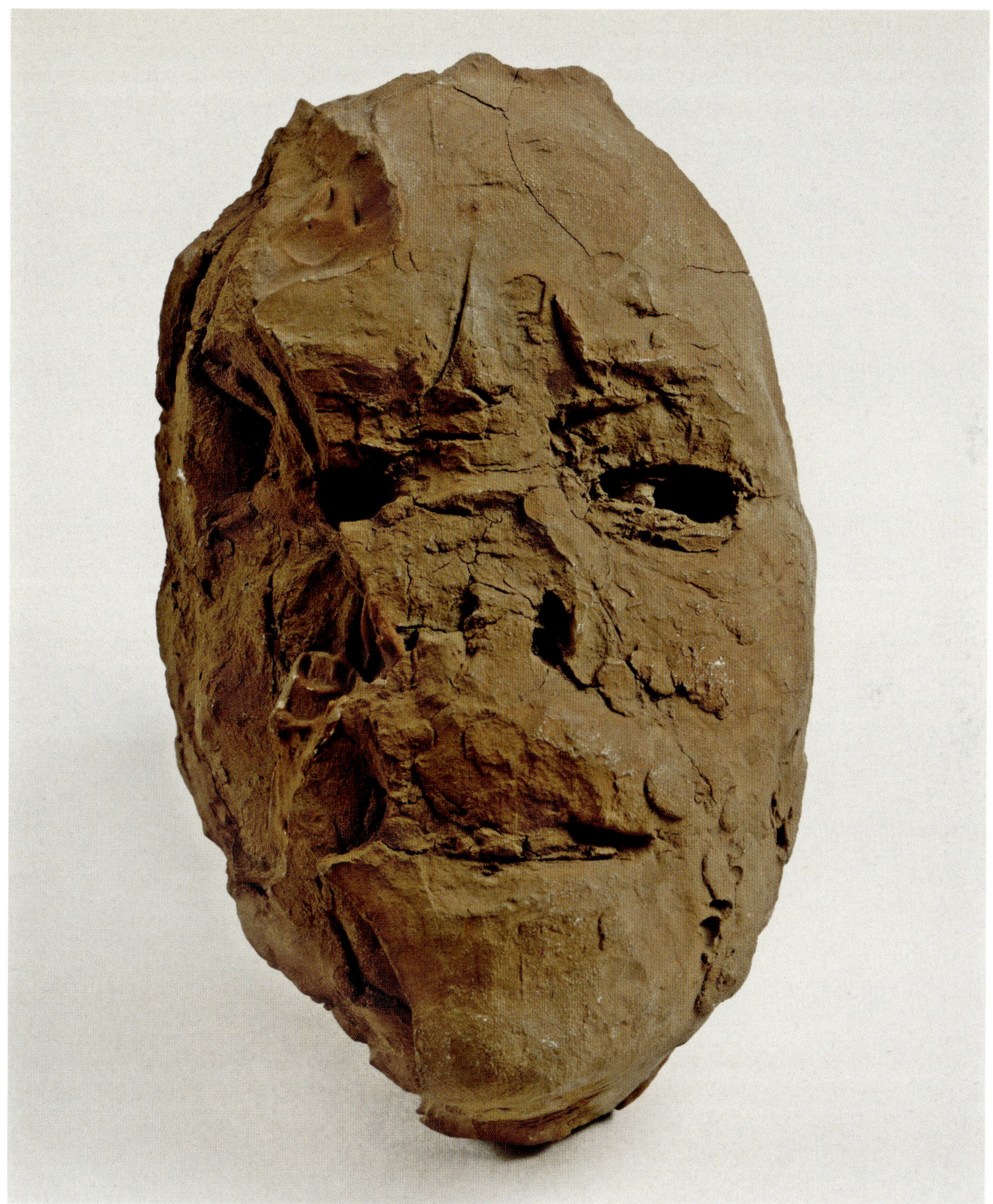

▷ 29   **Auguste Rodin**   Hanako   1907/08, terracotta, Musée Rodin, Paris

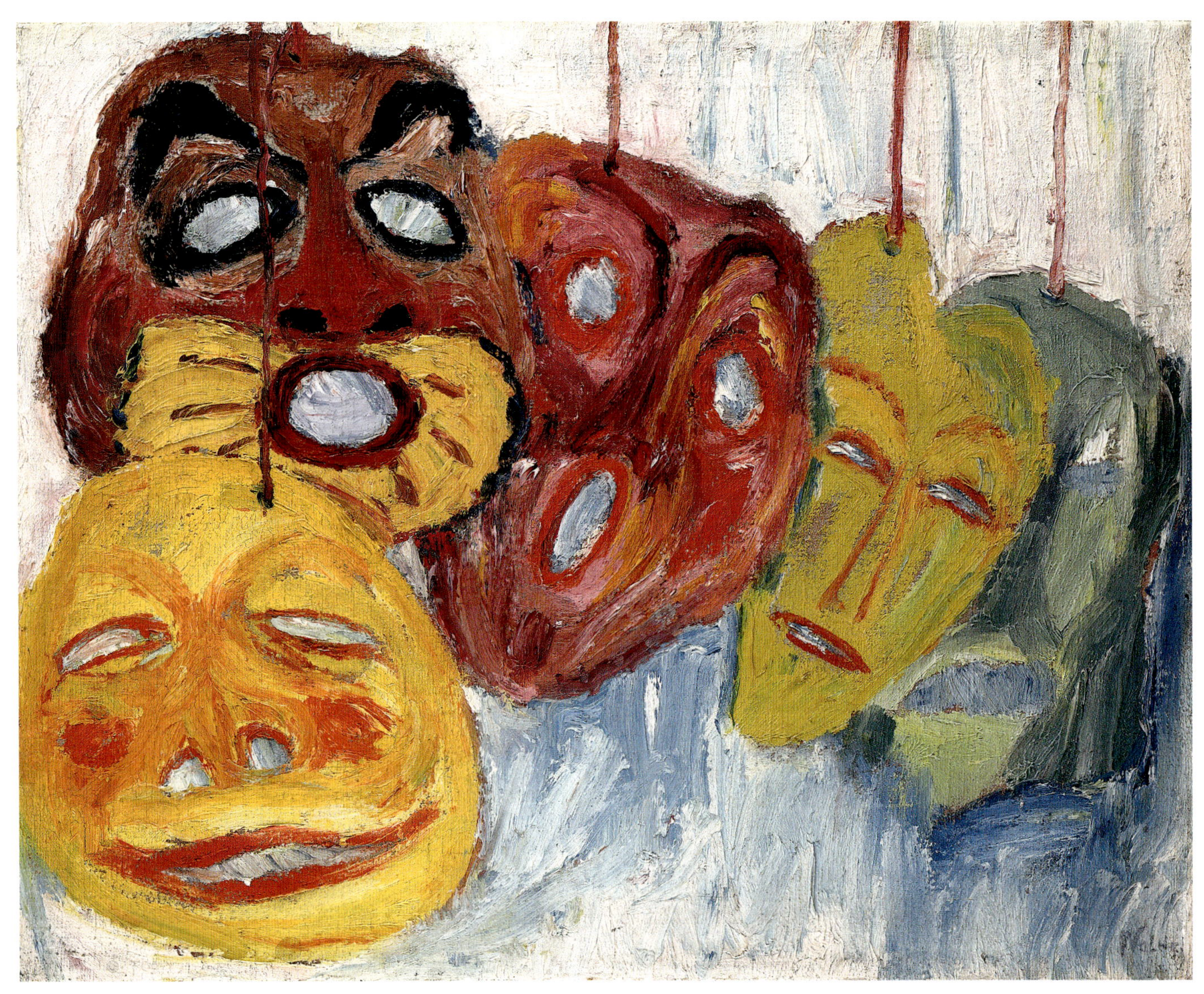

▷ 30   **Emil Nolde**   Still Life with Masks I
1911, oil on canvas, Nolde Stiftung, Seebüll

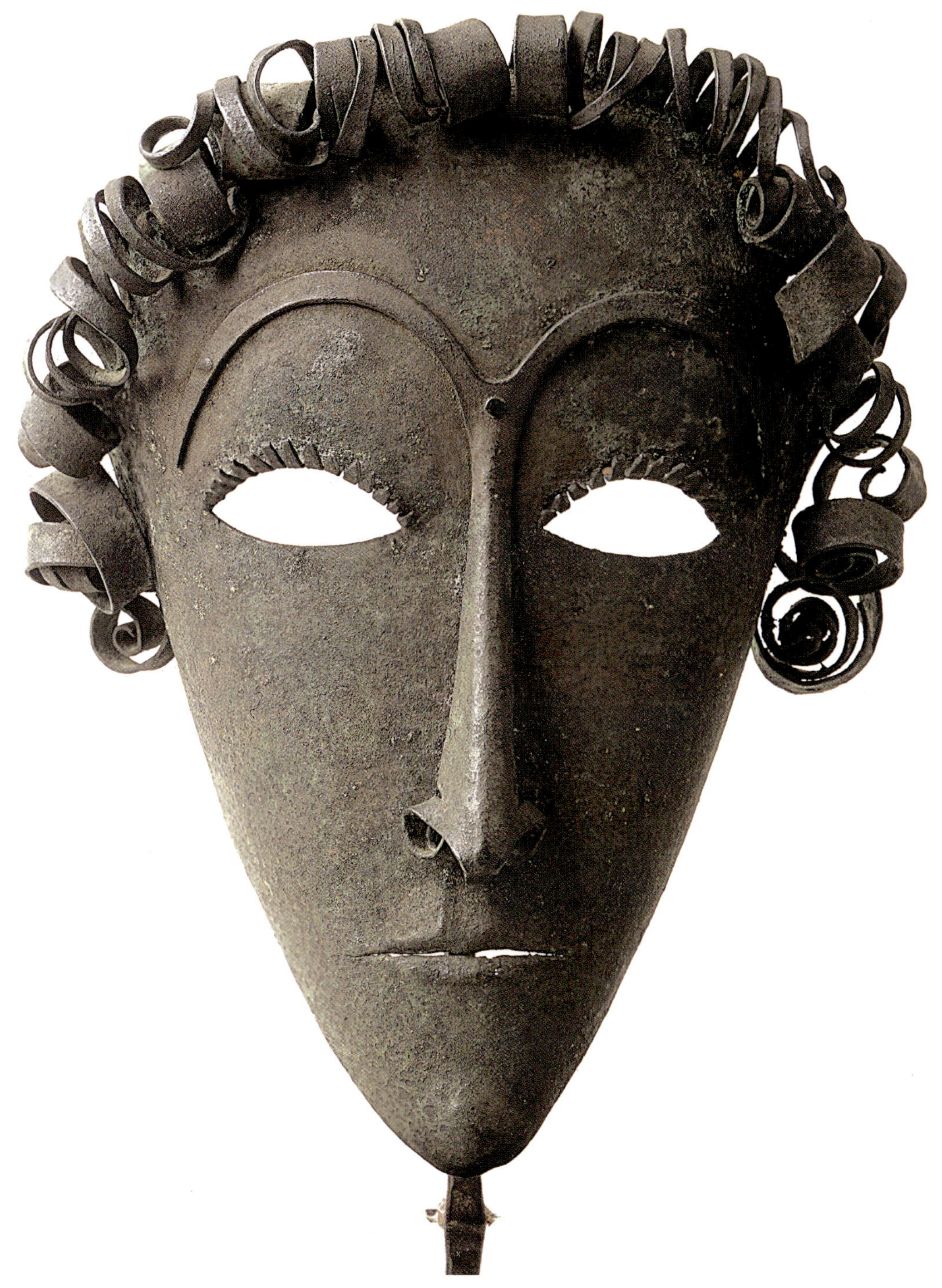

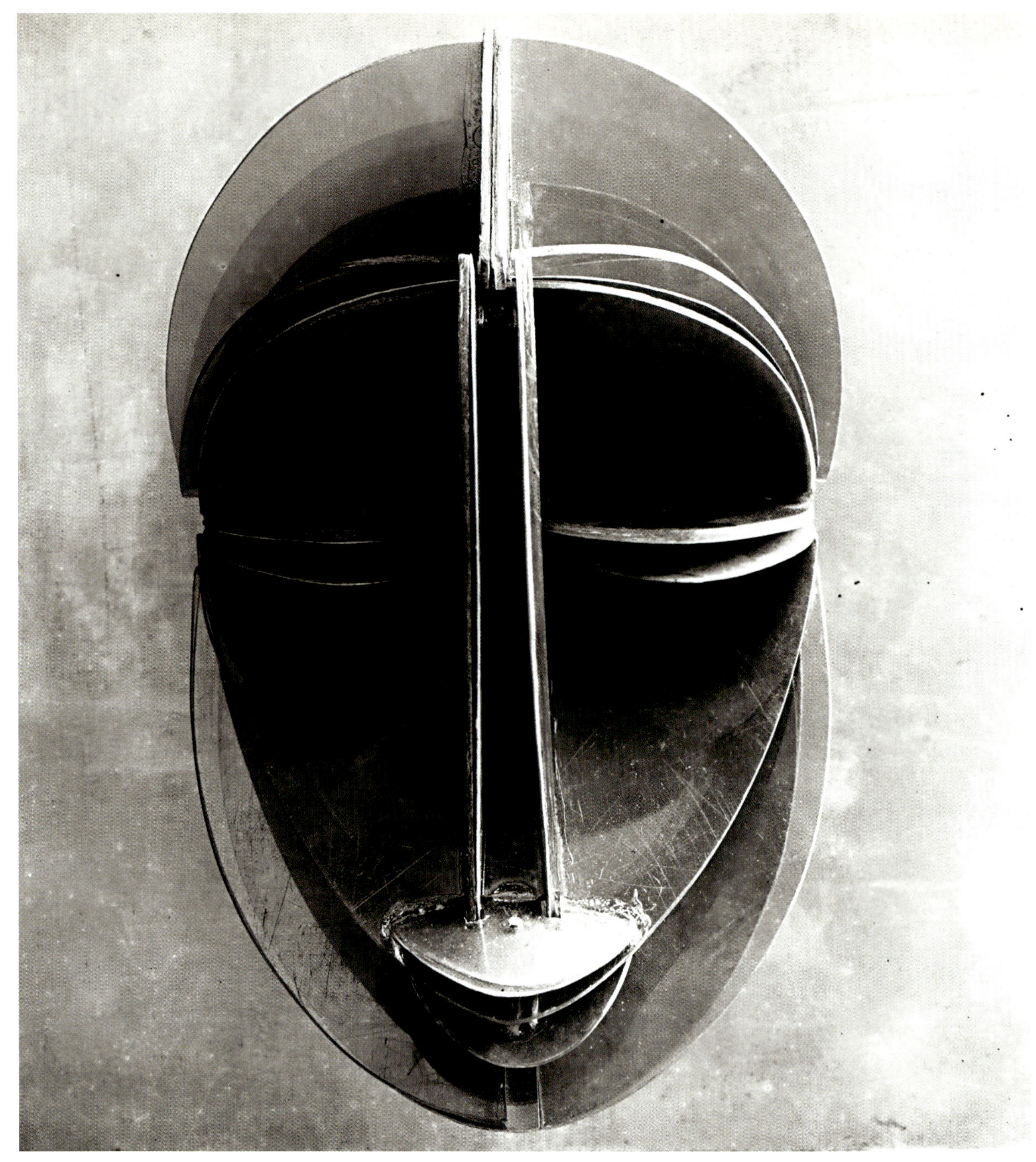

▷ 32   Marc Vaux   Mask by Antoine Pevsner
1923, photograph, modern copy of a glass plate,
Musée National d'Art Moderne – Centre Georges-Pompidou, Paris

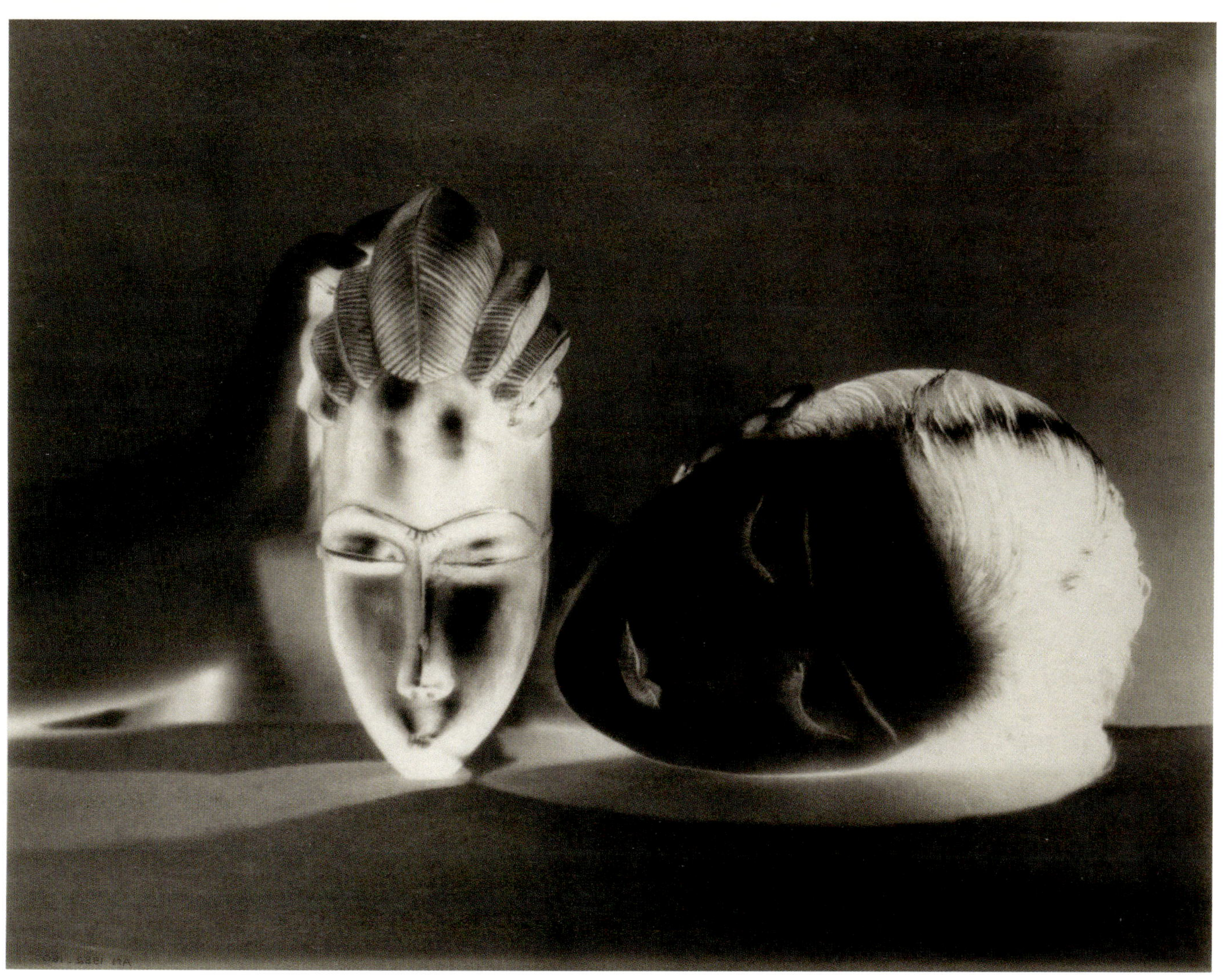

▷ 33   Man Ray   Black and White
1926, gelatin-silver print on baryte-free paper,
Musée National d'Art Moderne – Centre Georges-Pompidou, Paris

This book is published in conjunction with the exhibition
Masks. Metamorphoses of the Face. From Rodin to Picasso
Institut Mathildenhöhe Darmstadt, March 8th – June 7th, 2009

Audio CD
Conception: Ralf Beil
Editors: Ralf Beil, Mandana Edjtemai, Katharina Siegmann
Texts: Ralf Beil, Sabine Beil, Mandana Edjtemai, Hildegard Frübis, Nicole Grom, Anne Lepski,
Katja Molis, Ada Raev, André Ruo, Katharina Siegmann, Tanja Steinmetz, Annette Windisch
English Translations: Stephen Wright
Narrators: Brian Mc Credie, Fabian v. Klitzing, Hilary Owers, Anette Röser
Producer: soundgarden audioguidance GmbH
Director: Sabine Knapp
CD production: KMS Kafitz Medienservice GmbH, Elsdorf-Heppendorf

CD Booklet
Graphic design: KOMA AMOK, Stuttgart
Production: Stefanie Langner
Copyeditor: Alix Sharma
Typeface: Monotype Grotesque (Frank Hinman Pierpont)
Paper: LuxoSamtoffset, 170 g/m²
Reproductions: Weyhing digital, Ostfildern
Printing and binding: Kösel GmbH & Co. KG, Altusried
Published by:
Hatje Cantz Verlag, Zeppelinstraße 32, 73760 Ostfildern, Germany
Phone +49 711 4405-200, Fax +49 711 4405-220, www.hatjecantz.com

ISBN 978-3-7757-2416-6 (English)
ISBN 978-3-7757-2391-6 (German)

Printed in Germany

Cover illustration: Arnold Böcklin, *Shield with Medusa's Head,* after 1887, Musée d'Orsay, Paris

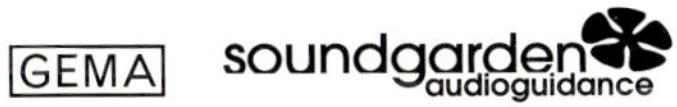

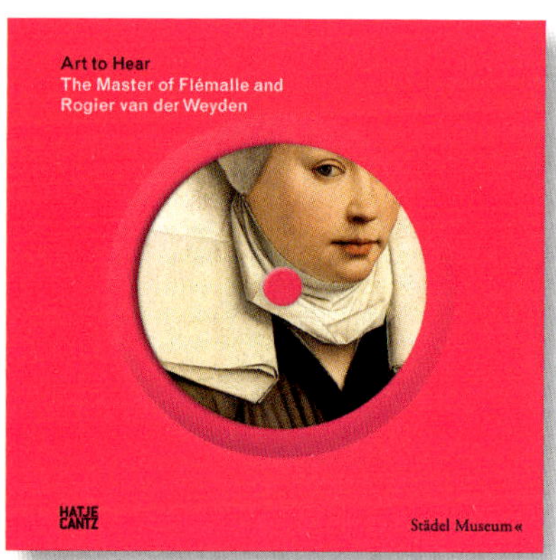
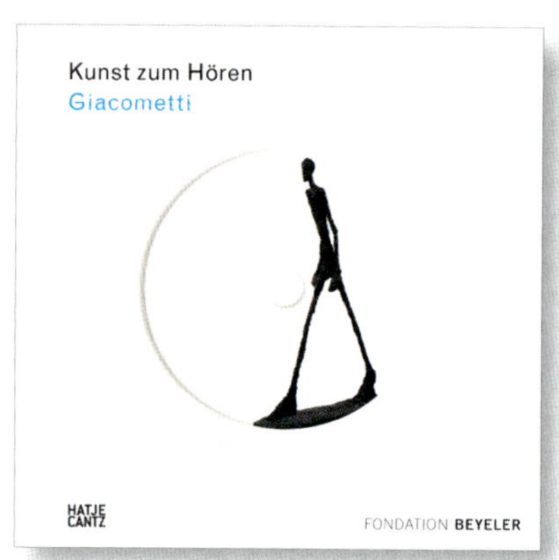
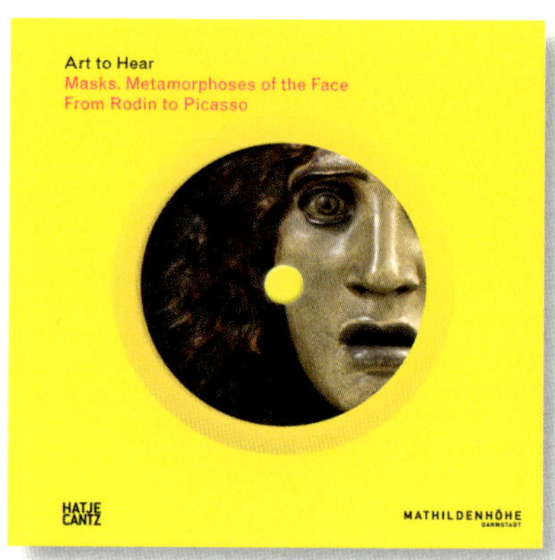

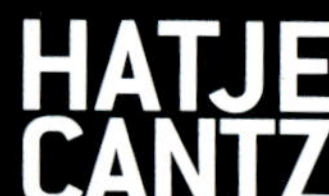
HATJE
CANTZ